Renteria

One Man's Healing from Cancer

HARRY S. DE CAMP

FLEMING H. REVELL COMPANY
OLD TAPPAN, NEW JERSEY

Scripture quotations identified RSV are from the Revised Standard Version of the Bible, copyrighted 1946, 1952, © 1971 and 1973.

Unless otherwise identified, Scripture quotations in this book are from the King James Version.

Some names in this book have been changed to protect the privacy of the individuals concerned.

Library of Congress Cataloging in Publication Data

DeCamp, Harry S.
One man's healing from cancer.

Includes bibliographical references.
1. Bladder—Cancer—Patients—New Jersey—Biography.
2. Christian life—1960- . 3. DeCamp, Harry S.
I. Title.
RC280.B5D43 1983 362.1'9699436 [B] 83-4444
ISBN 0-8007-1354-0

Published by Fleming H. Revell Company

Printed in the United States of America

I would like to dedicate this book to my good wife Bess, my daughter Judy, and my two little granddaughters, Holly and Heidi. Without their love, understanding, and cooperation this book would never have been started. I shall love them all forever.

With grateful thanks to my good friend, William Deerfield, skilled editor and writer, for his assistance in the preparation of this book.

Contents

"Therefore I tell you, whatever you ask in prayer, believe that you receive it, and you will."

Mark 11:24 RSV

Introduction

Harry DeCamp, the author of this highly inspirational book, is an unusual and remarkable man. In fact, in my personal opinion, he is one whom Almighty God has used to demonstrate anew His mercy and His power over disease. Harry was considered a terminal case but, remarkably, he found the healing power in full measure. He imaged a healing process and so he was healed of his disease.

That God was central to the process, Harry has never doubted for an instant. And the divine intervention that returned him to health from the brink of death was so unmistakable that only an arrogant and totally cynical person would attempt to deny it. And such denial is futile in the presence of the facts, for he was and remains healed. His total health is factual, whereas before he was marked for death by all medical standards. Now, by the same standards, he is a healthy, vigorous, happy and completely believing man.

When the disease struck him, Harry DeCamp was an honorable man who believed in morality, in the Bible and in the Christian religion in a nominal way. But he was not an avid and committed Christian, nor a church member. All of which proves that the power, the marvelous healing power, is reserved for those who have the capacity to believe. Belief is the answer and Harry believed in full measure. Undiluted, pure faith was his. As a result he received, on the basis of the scriptural promise: "According to your faith be it unto you." And as a result he has written this book which offers hope to everyone concerned with cancer.

I know Harry DeCamp as a personal friend. What he describes in his book as happening to him is true to the smallest detail. It actually occurred as he tells it. And if this marvelous happening can occur in the experience of one human being, as it did for Harry, the assumption surely is that the same healing can be repeated in the lives of others.

Harry DeCamp's experience is a spiritual, scientific breakthrough of healing power. He will, I believe, go down in the history of the healing process as an outstanding example of the incredible and gracious grace of God the Creator, demonstrating the power of God as a recreator.

Norman Vincent Peale

One Man's Healing from Cancer

1

The Wave

"Deep calleth unto deep at the noise of thy water-spouts; all thy waves and thy billows are gone over me."

Psalms 42:7

I sipped the Scotch and water slowly, letting the smooth liquid roll around in my mouth before I swallowed. It was quality stuff, and I wanted to savor it. I looked at the tall green bottle in front of me on the bar and read the label aloud: "Glenfiddich." I'd never heard of it; an odd sounding name, but I liked it. *Glenfiddich,* I repeated to myself.

"Where in the world did you ever hear of this brand?" I asked my buddy Ralph, who was sitting alongside of me at the bar.

"I ran across it in Scotland, when I was on a sales trip," he replied. "You really like it, Harry?"

"I *love* it!" I said, clapping him on the shoulder and taking another swallow.

"It is good stuff," Ralph said, tilting his glass to the light and swirling it. "It's sipping whiskey."

Ralph Thomas is a globe-trotting salesman for a firm that manufactures laboratory equipment, and he is something of a connoisseur of fine liquor. That raw, overcast day in April 1976, he and I were lunching and drinking at Bahrs, our favorite watering hole. Bahrs, one of the finest seafood restaurants on the East Coast, sprawls out on the shore of the Shrewsbury River in Highlands, New Jersey, where the Shrewsbury empties into Sandy Hook Bay.

Being that it was Saturday and the skies overcast, the place was full. The subdued murmur of voices drifted in from the spacious, dark-paneled dining room, behind the big circular bar. From the dining room, guests could look out on a bobbing forest of masts—one of the advantages of Bahrs is that boats can dock at the restaurant's private dock, for the convenience of hungry, thirsty weekend skippers.

The tantalizing aroma of fried seafood made me realize how hungry I was. We had already downed three drinks on empty stomachs, and I had a pleasant glow. We were drinking more than we should, cheered on by our affable, rotund bartender, Jimmy.

As if reading my thoughts, Jimmy leaned over the bar and said in a confidential tone: "Har, we have some nice soft-shell crabs today—big and really soft. Want to try some?"

I fixed him with a slightly-out-of-focus, are-you-kidding look, because Jimmy knew better than anybody that if there's one thing Harry DeCamp can never get enough of, it's soft-shell crabs. "Are there *two* on the platter for lunch?" I asked.

"There are for you, old buddy," Jimmy replied, as he went to call the order in. I settled back, sipping my Scotch. Life was great! I felt very comfortable. No wonder—my good friend sharing his knowledge of imported Scotch with me, and Jimmy always letting me know when the good crabs were in. Heck, life wasn't great—it was beautiful!

My wife Bess and I are lifelong residents of nearby West Long Branch, where I was a partner in a successful general insurance agency, and where also I had been active in local politics for years. I was even president—if you care to dignify the position with such a title—of the local chapter of the International Order of Old Duffers. (Well, not old *Duffers* really; the name we gave ourselves refers to legitimacy of birth, or, more correctly, *illegitimacy.*) It is a world wide organization of businessmen who get together for no loftier purpose than to eat, drink, and be merry—very merry. We held our meetings at Bahrs.

Jimmy brought out our platters, each containing two, big beautiful soft crabs, with french fries and coleslaw. Ralph and I sat there, eating and drinking, and having a ball. "Give us another round, Jimmy, okay?" I asked, midway through my second crab. "Let's try some pink vermouth. It'll go good with the crabs."

"You got it, buddy," Jimmy said, pouring the drinks.

"Hey, Ralph," I said, "you should have been here the other night. I got Kenny Bahrs real good."

Ralph cocked an eyebrow, as he pushed a forkful of fries into his mouth. "What happened, Har?"

I began to laugh. "Jimmy, tell Ralph what happened, will you? You remember, Kenny was at the service bar and the old guy and his wife were sitting behind Bess and me?"

"Oh, yeah!" Jimmy grinned. "There must have been fifty customers in the dining room that night. Harry was having dinner with Bess, right near the service bar.

"Anyway, Harry sends his drink back—got the wrong thing. He tells the waitress to tell Kenny *who* it's for, like he's some big shot. So the waitress tells Kenny and he looks up and says, 'For *who*? For that old Duffer over there?'

"Now there's this real old gent sitting with his missus, right behind Harry and Bess. Guy must have been in his late eighties, right, Harry? Anyway, the old guy says to Kenny, 'Who are you calling an old Duffer?' And the old guy's wife is almost falling off her chair in shock.

"Ken's as red as a beet, 'cause everybody's looking now. 'I was talking about that bald-headed man in front of you!' Now everybody's laughing. 'We got this club,' Kenny says, 'it's called . . .' and he's fumbling all around for his Old Duffers card, and he can't find it! And he looks at Harry for some help. But this clown here looks away, like he don't know Ken!

" 'Harry, show him your card, will you?' Kenny is pleading. So Harry says, 'What card?' The dining room's roaring now.

"So Bess says to Har, 'Harry, if you don't help Kenny right now, I'm getting up and walking out!' So, under duress, Har had to explain things to the old gent and his wife."

Then Jimmy swiped at the bar with his cloth, indicating the story was done. "Is Kenny talking to you yet, Har?"

"Sure . . ." I replied. "But, Ralph, the upshot was that the old gent wanted to join the Old Duffers on the spot!"

"Oh, is that all?" Ralph asked, looking at the two of us who were almost purple laughing, as if we were lunatics. "I've heard better."

"Come on, Ralph, it's a *great* story!" I said, suddenly feeling foolish, because we'd gotten carried away. I looked at my watch.

"Say, we'd better get out of here; it's almost 2:30!" Bess and Ralph's wife were out with some of the other wives; the "lunch bunch" they called themselves. Their routine was to go shopping on Saturday and have lunch together, while Ralph and I drank ours. But we didn't like to overdo it and get the girls mad at us.

Zipping my coat against the raw sea air, I made my way to my car, with Ralph trailing a few steps behind. I thought the fresh air would clear my head, but I was wrong. As I slid behind the wheel, I was still fuzzy. "Hey, Ralph . . . I think we drank our quota for today," I announced, as we started down Ocean Avenue.

"Would you believe, *more* than our quota?" he laughed.

I had had a brief bout with heavy drinking in the 1940s, but now I was strictly a weekend drinker. Unless I was taking an important client to lunch, I never drank during business hours. I had long ago made it a rule never to let a client or associate or friend smell liquor on my breath during business hours. It was forbidden in the insurance business. On those rare occasions when a business deal required luncheon drinks, I would immediately call it a day and head for home. But weekends were for unwinding and having fun—which I was about to have some of now.

"Let's stop and climb the seawall and take some pictures," I suggested. "I have my camera with me."

"All right with me," Ralph said. He probably would have agreed to anything at that stage of the game.

We had just had a bad Northeaster, and the wind was still blowing hard, as we entered the ocean front area. After two or three days, that wind can really rile the Atlantic, which is why this section of the coast is protected by a huge seawall, its rocks weighing several tons each. The waves were striking the wall with thundering booms, leaping over it and deluging the roadway. Before long the road would be closed to all traffic until the sea subsided.

Pulling off the road I parked in front of the big summer homes that stood boarded and blank, like blind sentinels facing the ocean, waiting for their summer owners—known as "Indians" to us shore natives. Ralph and I trotted across to the seawall, tiptoeing unsteadily through the small lakes forming on the road.

You'd think that having been born and raised in the area, I would have, by the age of 66, taken the ocean for granted. But not so. I have always loved the sea, and I still do, particularly after a storm like this one, when it is seething and restless, like some huge, white-maned beast, with paws that could slap fifty-ton boulders from the seawall, scattering them across the road like so much gravel.

On just such a raw, stormy day as this in the wake of another Northeaster back in 1929 I had had a bad experience, only a mile or so down this beach. I was a rugged young lifeguard of 19 then. I was trying to save a man who had foolishly ventured into the roaring surf and as I struggled to keep his head above water, we were caught in what is known as a seapuss, a kind of tidal whirlpool that pulled us a quarter mile up the coast. I had staggered ashore with my burden at Monmouth Beach, and collapsed on the sand, where the first aid squad found us. The man I was attempting to save had actually suffered a stroke while in my arms and was dead. I had seen the light go out of his eyes as I struggled through the surf to the shore.

When we had been swept up in the seapuss, a friend had raced to my home in West Long Branch to tell my stunned parents that I had drowned. Later, when they saw me coming up the driveway, my mother almost fainted.

But now, almost forty years later, as Ralph and I scampered up the weathered wooden steps to the platform atop the seawall, that grim experience that had happened so close by never crossed my mind; I had forgotten my near encounter with death and the horror of it in a dying man's eyes.

"This is a great spot, Ralph," I said. "See, the waves are breaking on either side of us here." Ralph didn't look too enthusiastic. I busied myself framing and shooting pictures of the waves as Ralph stood there shivering in the steady Easterly wind. I consider myself a fair photographer; samples of my work grace one wall of our living room, most of them subtly lighted pictures of my two granddaughters.

The waves were spectacular that day, fifteen to twenty feet high. I took picture after picture of the huge, roaring, foamy giants as they rolled in, smashing against the seawall. Minutes passed. *Click . . . click . . .* the shutter of my Nikon played a neat counterpoint to the bass drum boom of the surf. I was totally absorbed in my picture-taking. How else could I have failed to see *the wave?*

It was a massive wall that rose higher and higher as it careened toward us. I could *see* its gigantic proportions through the viewfinder, but somehow it didn't register as anything but fascinating. The inner wall of that monster wave was covered with intriguing patterns; strange blocks and squares I had never seen in a wave before.

Wow! What a shot! I thought. I held back, as the white

wall moved inexorably toward the seawall, until just the right moment. Then I hit the trigger. . . .

Almost simultaneously, roaring whiteness struck the rocks and splashed over my head and shoulders and back. I gasped, staggering sideways; then, white coils of water pulled at my knees and ankles before slithering off the wall into the maelstrom below.

Stunned and sputtering, I looked over to where Ralph stood, drenched and dripping. At least we were both on our feet. It was ridiculous! Me, with a lifetime of experience in the ways of the ocean, caught off guard! It was a wonder we hadn't been knocked off that twenty-foot wall into the ocean or onto the road. Either way it would have been disastrous; I wasn't a young, rugged lifeguard anymore.

"Hey, old salt!" Ralph burbled. "You really know how to pick a dry spot! That was a direct hit . . . on us!" He was not as wet as I.

Chagrined, considerably sobered, and soaked to the skin, I sloshed off the rocks and across the road to the car. I shed my dripping coat and wiped the camera off as best I could, hoping the salt water hadn't penetrated it. With Ralph shivering beside me, I drove silently to my house, where he picked up his car and continued on his way.

Our comfortable little house on Hendrickson Place, which Bess and I had built in the early 1950s, was dark and quiet as I pulled up. Bess hadn't gotten home yet. Ordinarily, I hated coming home to an empty house, but today I was glad of it. Bess would have chewed me out but good as I made my half-drunk, wet and dripping entrance.

I went immediately to the bathroom and stripped off my wet clothes, wringing them out and hanging them in the furnace room. Then I took a nice hot shower and put some dry things on.

In about an hour Bess came in from her shopping expedition. She listened, a little annoyed, as I told her about our escapade; then she asked, "When are you men going to grow up? You're worse than a couple of kids!"

Bess was right! I was just a big kid. Or worse—I was a silly grown man. But, hey, I had worked hard all my life. I had raised a daughter, had a successful business. So . . . I overdid things a bit. I just wanted to have a good time while I could. What was wrong with that?

I closed the bathroom door. Those drinks were having their effect. The water in the toilet bowl had a pinkish color to it. Strange. *Boy, that vermouth goes right through you* I thought as I washed my hands. In a little while Bess called me to dinner, and I thought nothing more about it. We had a pleasant evening, but I was tired after the eventful afternoon, so I went to bed about eleven.

I awoke the next morning at 8:30, with a slight hangover. I don't eat a big breakfast, so I sipped a glass of milk and read the Sunday papers. It was a pleasant, lazy day.

We didn't go to church. Ever. Not that Bess wouldn't have liked to. She believed in God and had even taught Sunday school in her youth, and had made sure our daughter Judy went to Sunday school, too. But because I didn't go to church, over the years she gradually stopped going. We had long since stopped having discussions about it. Bess knew it was no good discussing something with me once my mind was made up. Especially church.

Actually, I had a great dislike for church people. All my life I had been meeting what I called "church-ified" types, and most of them were smug hypocrites as far as I could see. There were exceptions of course. My grandfather, on my father's side, had been a minister and he was a decent man, I'm told. I don't know. I never met him. And then there was my mother. She was a devout Christian and churchgoer and had instructed me in the faith as best she could. But somehow I got the idea early on that religion was all right for some other guy, but not me. I didn't need it.

And when I looked at many so-called Christians, I knew it wasn't for me. They'd take advantage of other people; they'd do you dirty in business. And when they weren't outright dishonest, they were hard-nosed and judgmental.

You'd never catch one of them in a bar having a good time. And they'd point their bony fingers at anyone else who did.

So, on a given Sunday morning, if anybody were to tell me that I'd have to put on a suit and tie and go to the local Methodist or Presbyterian church and stand with a hymnbook in my hand, singing with a bunch of old biddies, my reaction would have been one of total *revulsion.* I was a free spirit; nobody in that tribe was going to hamper me.

It wasn't that I didn't believe in God. I did. He had even helped me out of a few scrapes in my life, like that incident on the beach. (Not that I gave Him credit for it at the time!) But He was a little like a distant, kindly old uncle whom I didn't visit very often. To my mind, God certainly had nothing whatever to do with the established church.

That was why I was lounging at home that Sunday morning reading the papers and watching exhibition baseball on TV.

About four o'clock I went to the bathroom.

Clots—thick red clots the color of claret were suddenly floating in the bowl as I urinated. I was shocked and a little scared.

"Bess . . . Bess . . . !" I called.

"What is it, Hon?" she answered from the kitchen. "I'm busy. . . ."

"I want you to come in here and see something!" I was unable to take my eyes off the bloody water. *Something was wrong with me, but Bess would know what to do. She always managed to make things right . . . somehow.*

She came in and looked over my shoulder. "Oh, Harry!" she said softly, sucking in her breath. I told her about the pink vermouth in the toilet bowl the previous evening.

"Oh, Harry, come on!" she said, her voice shrilling slightly, as it always did when she was anxious or frightened. "How can you be dumb enough to believe that you can drink pink wine and it will pass through you still pink? The body chemicals change it! That's *blood!* I think we should call the doctor!"

Bess hurried to the living room to dial our family physician, Dr. Demaree, while I stood there debating about whether I should flush the evidence away.

"He's not in," she said anxiously, as I came out of the bathroom. "They'll give him the message to call us. . . ."

While we waited for the doctor to call, we ate dinner. Neither of us was hungry. "It's probably a kidney stone, or an infection of some kind," Bess said, picking at her food and not looking at me. "Does it hurt at all, Har?"

"No . . ." I replied truthfully. That was the strange part; I felt no discomfort. Surely if it were something serious I'd be in pain.

"It's not bad enough having Vince so sick in the hospital," Bess said, "now you're sick too!" My brother-in-law, Vince, was in Monmouth Medical Center, critically ill with cancer.

"Honey," I said, trying to be patient, "you've got me in a hospital bed already. It's probably only a little infection, like you said." Bess said nothing but pushed back her chair and took my uneaten dinner to the garbage pail.

Within an hour Dr. Demaree called. "What's the matter, Harry?" he asked in his soft, professional tone, the one designed to keep patients and their spouses calm in a crisis. While Bess hovered near, I explained the situation to him.

"Harry, I want you to call a urologist the first thing tomorrow." Giving me the doctor's name, his voice was suddenly crisp and authoritative. "Now, you've got to insist that he see you immediately. Okay? Have him call me after you're through."

Bess busied herself getting the overnight bag and hospital effects together, scolding me gently all the while. "See what happens to you when you don't pay attention to me? See what happens when you drink too much? Now, tomorrow first thing, put a urine specimen in a bottle. We want to show it to the specialist. I'm sure he'll put you in the hospital right away."

Bess's mother had been a nurse, so she had grown up

well-versed in the ways of doctors and medical things in general. Although I thought she was overreacting, I said nothing. Suddenly she stopped folding the pajamas she was about to stuff in the bag and looked at me. "Oh, Hon . . . you big, overgrown ape, you!" she said, her voice cracking slightly. She rushed to me and hugged me tightly.

"Now, you get a good night's sleep," she admonished, kissing me tenderly on the cheek, ". . . and don't worry about a thing."

While I was getting ready for bed I could hear her talking softly to our daughter Judy on the phone. Judy lived on the other side of town with her husband Rick and our two granddaughters, Holly and Heidi. Bess was telling Judy about me thinking the blood was pink vermouth. *Well, maybe I hadn't wanted to admit it was anything else,* I thought. *I'll never live that down. . . .*

Later, I lay in the dark, wondering what it could possibly be. I felt fine, but the sight of all that blood in the toilet was a little frightening. Turning over and plumping the pillow I thought, *This specialist will knock it out with a little antibiotics . . . whatever it is.* I slept soundly.

Early the next morning I went into the bathroom with the specimen bottle. I was shocked. The bright red liquid didn't have the appearance of ordinary blood, but was thick, viscous.

"I don't like the looks of that at all!" Bess said, thoroughly alarmed. "It looks like *plasma!*"

I called the urologist, whose manner was quite impressive. We got a 2:00 P.M. appointment.

We arrived with the specimen bottle and overnight bag in hand. The doctor took one look at the contents of the bottle, and without saying a word to either of us, reached over and dialed the hospital. Identifying himself, he said, "I want to reserve a room for a Mr. Harry DeCamp. Yes. . . . Right away. Yes. . . ."

He hung up and said, "Mr. DeCamp, you're going into the hospital, right now. Monmouth Medical. Okay?" Bess and I exchanged quick glances. She had that I-told-you-so-Harry-but-you-wouldn't-believe-me expression on her face.

"Are you ready?" the doctor said, standing up. I could hardly believe it. I didn't *feel* sick, yet this doctor was going to put me in a hospital bed. I mean, he hadn't even examined me.

"Yes," I replied, grinning and feeling slightly foolish.

The doctor frowned. "Mr. DeCamp, don't get upset. We just want to get a good look."

"Harry, listen to the doctor," Bess was saying. "He knows what he's talking about."

No way! I was thinking. *She thinks it's serious. Maybe for somebody else, but not for me!*

But something in Bess's face made my flippant smile fade. It was fear.

The Medical Center was just a short walk from the doctor's office. So before I knew it, they had me checked in and propped up in one of those hard hospital beds. A battery of nurses were poking me, sticking me, questioning me, while Bess hung my clothes neatly in my locker and then fussed with my night table, arranging my personal things. I tried joking with the nurses, but Bess kept shushing me, telling me to behave.

Bess seemed calm enough now, which was not at all surprising. She tends to be a worry wart before things happen. Now that I was being taken care of, she was able to handle things better. She wasn't even unduly alarmed when we were told that my bladder would be examined in the morning and cauterized (burned) to stop the hemorrhaging.

"Now don't worry, Hon," she assured me, solicitously stroking my brow. "It's nothing serious; they can handle this easily, I'm sure." Then she kissed me quickly on the cheek, squeezed my hand, and was gone.

By now I wasn't buying Bess's too eager reassurances. What was it somebody said about the lady protesting too much? After supper that night I tried watching TV, but thoughts, crazy thoughts, kept running through my mind in wild confusion. *Looks like plasma. . . . What is it? This could be serious, Harry. Hon, it's nothing serious. . . . Some infection . . . they'll knock it out. . . . Why such heavy bleeding? We'll cauterize it. . . .*

I slept fitfully, wishing I was home in my own bed. The night was endless. Nurses rustled in and out of the dimly lit room in their starchy uniforms from time to time, ordering me to take pills from little paper containers, or taking my temperature or blood pressure.

Before the sun was quite up, they were prepping me for the medical "procedure," as they called it. A nurse came in and jabbed me with a needle that was supposed to make me feel totally relaxed, but didn't. Then two orderlies, with wrinkled green uniforms, came and hauled me onto a cart for the ride to the operating room.

In that room I lay staring up at the big overhead light, when someone leaned over and stuck a needle in my hand. Out I went.

I was coming awake, but was still very drowsy and comfortable. Above me was Bess's face, her dark eyes staring intently down at me. *How pretty Bess is!* I thought. *How really pretty! She can't be sixty-two and look so pretty. . . . I'm sixty-six, and she's four years younger. . . .* Some part of my brain was alert. Dreamily I contemplated her face: close-cut dark hair, framing a perfect oval. And deep dark eyes. *That's my Bess!*

Melvina . . . she had been christened Melvina, but everyone called her "Bess." It is our wedding day . . . how lovely she looks. The minister is saying, "Will you, Melvina, take this man. . . ." And the church is buzzing: "Melvina . . . who is that?" They don't know her real name. . . . How funny!

The thought makes me smile weakly. *Bess turns to me to say "I do," but she is frowning and anxious. Oh . . . yes, now I remember, I'm in the hospital, not the church. . . .*

"How did it go, Hon?" Bess said softly. I was just out of the recovery room. Weakly I nodded my head, managing to make an "okay" sign with my fingers. She smiled, as if satisfied and then stroked my head gently, as I slipped into a sound sleep.

The next morning the urologist came to see me. He said they had examined my bladder with a cystoscope and had discovered two spots the size of quarters. I was relieved to learn they had cauterized them to stop the bleeding, as they said they would.

It didn't hurt at all, but they had placed a catheter in me, as a drain. *Now at least I can get better and go home,* I thought. *No more bleeding.*

"Harry . . ." the doctor was saying, "I took a biopsy, which we've sent to Washington. Nothing to worry about right now. We should have the results back in little over a week."

"A biopsy?" I asked with an incredulous grin. "That's for *cancer,* isn't it, doctor? Well . . . you're wasting your time and mine. It'll come back negative, believe me."

"Let's hope so," he said, returning the smile.

"Why can't I go home? I can wait for the biopsy results there as well as here. Right?" He was shaking his head "no" the whole time I was talking.

"Harry, I want you to get plenty of rest, and this is the best place for it," he advised, patting my leg. Then he turned and hurried from the room.

During the next seven days, Bess, Judy, and my relatives and friends were in and out to see me. Periodically, the nurses would appear to shoo part of the mob from my room. It was fun holding court and being the center of attention. I enjoyed that.

One afternoon during visiting hours, the doctor suddenly appeared in the doorway. There was a respectful silence in the room as he entered.

"Hello," he said to the group. There were murmured replies. "Uh . . . Harry, can I see you for a minute, outside?"

"Sure, Doc," I said, swinging my legs off the bed and

reaching for my slippers. "Be back in a minute, folks." I could feel Bess's eyes on me, as I padded toward the door—or rather, lurched—with my metal "tree" and its clanging intravenous bottle, plus my catheter bag.

The doctor seated himself in the hall and lit a cigarette. We exchanged small talk; I stood looking down at him, while holding my "tree." His face became curiously stiff, his voice serious. "Harry . . ." he began, "Harry . . . there is no easy way to tell you. You have cancer."

What? WHAT?

He raced on: "We found two spots on your bladder. They were the size of 25-cent pieces. We've stopped the bleeding, but the report has come back. They're malignant."

I looked at him. I heard him, but surely he was talking about someone else, not *me!* It was several minutes before it sank in.

I HAD CANCER!

A shiver ran through my body. Then the blood drained from my face in a rush. It seemed to plummet to my feet, making my stomach and legs feel strangely heavy, numb actually. Then it returned to my face and head in another rush. I was giddy. . . . *Cancer!*

All at once I felt calm, really calm and in total control. It was amazing. An instant earlier I had been on the verge of passing out, with my circulation running amok, and now . . . nothing. My sudden aplomb surprised me.

"Okay, doctor, let's go after it . . . clean it out of there in a hurry, shall we?" So calm and collected was I.

What's the matter with you? my mind screamed. *He just told you—YOU HAVE CANCER!* Still the calm persisted.

I walked back into my room and fumbled into bed. My visitors were still there, joking and making small talk. "What did he want, Hon?" Bess asked innocently. *Poor Bess.*

"He told me I have cancer of the bladder."

It was as if I had tossed a bomb into the group, but instead of an explosion, a startled stillness fell over the room.

After a few quiet minutes, my guests started making lame, silly excuses, as they practically dashed from the room. They ran like thieves. They acted as if the cancer might be catching!

Soon Bess and I were alone. "Oh, Harry!" she cried, her voice husky and her eyes suddenly full. Then she dropped on the bed beside me. Burying her head on my shoulder, she wept softly.

2

The Maverick

"Be not like a horse or a mule, without understanding, which must be curbed with bit and bridle, else it will not keep with you."

Psalms 32:9 RSV

Just before Bess put her head on my shoulder and began to cry, she leaned over and said something that really surprised me. "Har," she said, her voice husky, "we've had a good life together. We have a wonderful daughter, two lovely grandchildren. If this is the way the good Lord wants it, we'll just make the best of the time we have left."

"That's a fine thing to say!" I snorted. It was then she began to cry. As I patted her shoulder, trying to comfort her, I was thinking: *I'm not finished yet. After all, it's only cancer of the bladder. They can take care of that. No problem.*

But later that night, as I tried to sleep, Bess's words came back to me. *"We'll make the best of the time we have left."* How much time did I have? It's funny, but I had thought my life would go on and on, and now Bess was talking about it *ending.* I think it was Sigmund Freud who said that no man can ever really imagine his own death. That night, as I lay there alone, thinking, I could not believe I might die. The idea kept eluding me somehow. Death was something that always happened to others, something you read about or see in the movies or on TV. It couldn't touch me.

Between my denials on the one hand and my indignation on the other, all the grim brainwashing so thoroughly drilled into all of us by the media, concerning cancer, kept surfacing to torment me. The bottom line was: *cancer and death are synonymous. It's only a matter of time. Everybody knows that.*

My own brother-in-law, Vince, was in the same hospital at that very moment, in a very bad way with cancer. He wasn't expected to live. Not only Vince, but two of my good friends were also there. And both of them had cancer! Wasn't it only a few days earlier that I had visited all three ("making the rounds," I called it), standing there, hat in hand, or sitting telling jokes and making small talk, all the while feeling uncomfortable and sorry for them? The irony was incredible! While I had been pitying them, feeling vibrantly healthy myself, secretly, insidiously, the cells of my own body were going haywire.

In the darkness I looked over at the other bed in my semi-private room. It was empty. It stood there rigid, silent, its clinically white sheets softly piercing the gloom. I wondered what its occupant would be like . . . old, young? Happy, sour? Very ill, slightly ill . . . ?

I had been *born* in this very hospital. It was much smaller then, and was known as Monmouth Memorial. So long ago, a lifetime, really—March 16, 1910—sixty-six years and one month almost exactly. I had had the distinction of being the second biggest baby ever born there. I weighed in at fifteen and three-quarter pounds!

I was the youngest of eight children. As a baby, I may have been spoiled; frankly I don't remember. My dad was a stationary steam engineer at Chattle High School in Long Branch. He was an honest, hardworking man. The salt of the earth.

After a faulty start in life (twice I nearly died from bouts with scarlet fever and double pneumonia) I grew like a weed. I played all sports, but I was a lazy student. Back then it was just like today; they gave athletes a bit of preferential treatment, so I always got by. I loved sports so much that I deliberately stayed back a half year to play baseball—with the surreptitious blessings of the coach.

The spring I graduated from high school, I wasn't sure what I wanted to do, so I took that job as lifeguard at the Avenel Beach in Long Branch, for the summer. There would be plenty of time to decide what I wanted to do later on, or so I thought. There wasn't time, though. It was 1929.

On a Tuesday in October (Black Tuesday they were to call it), the stock market crashed, plunging the country into the Great Depression.

Dad was luckier than most; he worked for the board of education, so his job was safe. Still, he was paid in scrip, a kind of promissory note, only good locally. No one had much cash.

For a young man just entering the labor force, there was little or no work to be found. But I was strong and resourceful and had a good pair of hands. Without telling my parents, I started boxing as an amateur around the Jersey shore area and as far north as Newark.

The prize for winning was usually a brass watch casing, with a ten dollar bill folded inside in place of the watch works. I won several fights. I had to—I needed that prize money. I fought under the colorful name of Lefty Del Campo.

I was lucky not to get marked up; my parents would have raised a ruckus if they had known I was fighting in the ring for a few dollars. But in my last bout—my twentieth—I met a buzz saw. He hit me with everything but the ring posts. That night I was some sight when I arrived home. I stood there with a black eye, a split lip and a puffed ear, trying to explain to Mom that this was no big thing.

Mom began to cry. "Harry . . . no more fighting! Do you hear me? Just look at you! Dad! Come here and look at what your son's done to himself! Boxing! They've nearly killed him!"

If she thought that Dad would jump on me, she was

wrong. He didn't say much. I suspect he was secretly proud of me. Anyway, that ended my boxing career.

After that, I took a job as an electrician's helper on the Atlantic Highlands Bridge, which still spans the Shrewsbury River. But I was eventually laid off. Then I'd get a few days work here, a few there. Things were grim.

I asked Dad if I could work with him in the boiler room at the high school. "No. You're not cut out for that. I won't let you do it!" he growled. I kept after him until he relented.

It was back-breaking labor. We were up every morning at three and would go trudging through the frosty darkness to the school. First we'd shovel up the soft coal and pile it in front of the boilers. Then I'd have to scoop up the coal and heave it into the furnaces.

The furnaces were a good fifteen feet deep, with narrow iron doors. The first week my shovel hit the sides of the door four times out of five, sending soft coal flying in every direction but into the furnace. The force of the shovel striking the solid iron sent shock waves from my wrists to my shoulders. It really stung.

"Damn it all, Harry!" Dad would bellow. "You've got to heave it in *straight!*" Not only did you have to heave it in straight, you had to be ambidextrous, learning to throw it first from the right side of the door, and then from the left.

About mid-morning, I would take a fifteen-foot iron rod, run it into the furnace over a roller attached to the open doors, and break up the clinkers. Then with a long hoe, I'd push the live coals to the back, raking the clinkers to the front and onto the concrete floor. Next I'd hose it all down, then shovel the heavy clinkers into a wheelbarrow and push it up a 45-degree ramp, out of the building to the ash heap.

Dad tried to work me to death that winter. I still think he made it hard on me deliberately, hoping I'd quit. Come spring, he said again, "Harry, this is not for you." This time I believed him; it sure wasn't for me! Still, I was grateful for that work. It had paid $25 a week, which was very decent money in those hard times.

So I said goodbye to the boiler room and went back to being a lifeguard for the summer. In the fall of 1930 I took a job at a gas station.

At the time, my sister Hannah and her husband Chet used to invite me over. They were newly married. Hannah was always telling me how great it was to be married. I wasn't buying it though. I dated casually, but with times like they were, I wasn't about to do something stupid, like taking a wife and responsibilities.

One evening Hannah began talking seriously about a new friend of hers; "a very nice person," was the way she described her. Chet's nephew Harold had brought the girl to the house to have cinnamon toast one night, Hannah reported. The two girls had become fast friends.

"Why, Harry, do you know that Bess—that's her name, Bess. (Well, *actually* it's Melvina, but we all call her Bess.) Well, do you know she *never* had cinnamon toast before? She's the cutest thing! I'd really like you to meet her, Har. She's just turned sixteen."

"No thanks!" I snapped. And that was the end of that.

A week or so later I dropped by in the afternoon. We were sitting having coffee when Hannah jumped up and went to the window. After a few minutes she called me. "Harry, here's that girl I was telling you about! Come, quick!"

I went to the window. Hannah was smiling and waving down to a tall girl with dark hair, knotted in the back under a beret. She was passing the house with a bookbag over her shoulder. The girl smiled and waved back.

"Ah . . . she's not so hot!" I said, turning away.

Hannah wouldn't give up. On Saturday she called the house and said, "Harry, come on over. I've got to go into Asbury to meet Chet. He's working late at the store, and I want some company."

"Can't. I'm with my pal Herb."

"Well, bring him along, silly!"

When we got to Hannah's that girl was sitting in the living room, sipping tea. She was pretty all right, with a nice figure and with high aristocratic cheekbones. She was dark, though, almost like an Indian. I wondered if she were an Indian.

Hannah fell all over herself introducing us. "Harry played all sports in school, Bess; and he lifeguards in the summer."

"I've seen him around," Bess replied, clearly unimpressed by my credentials.

"Harry . . . Bess plays girls' soccer and basketball!" Hannah volunteered. Then, as if she had just thought of it, she added a bit too brightly, "Say! You kids have something in common. You both love sports!"

Bess and I looked at each other. Uncomfortably.

During the ride over to Asbury, Herb drove his car and Bess and I sat in the rumble seat. We hardly spoke, but her arm pressing against mine in the confined space felt good. It was then I noticed she had a very beautiful profile.

We picked Chet up at the clothing store where he worked and went for ice cream sodas. "Say, I've got an idea!" Hannah said, still trying. "Tommy Dorsey is at the Convention Hall Saturday night! Let's go dancing! Bess just loves to dance, don't you, Bess?"

Bess looked into her soda, poking at it with her straw. "Do you like to dance, Bess?" I asked, leaning forward a little across the table.

"I do like to . . ." she replied, looking at me suddenly with her piercing dark eyes.

Years later, Bess told me that she had thought I was good-looking, but conceited, when we first met. She liked my dark, wavy hair. But she wasn't particularly attracted to me. I must have really grown on her, because we began to see more and more of each other.

Of course, Bess's parents were quite strict with her. She had to be in at nine on weeknights. On Saturday she had a 10:00 P.M. curfew. In those days we didn't know anything about psychology or any of the things young people think are so important today. We didn't analyze one another; we were having too much fun for that. We were kind of innocent and naive. There was no such thing as premarital sex. You were lucky if you were able to steal a kiss or two on the front porch.

My job at the filling station ended in September 1934, and if anything, the Depression was deepening. There were no jobs to be had anywhere locally.

One day I saw an ad in the *Asbury Park Press.* An elderly couple from Long Branch were driving to California and needed a driver to spell them. California! I could almost see the palm trees, orange groves, and movie stars! I was sure there would be work out there. It was worth a try! And it would be exciting!

I talked it over with my parents. Reluctantly they agreed. Then I called the people who placed the ad and made an appointment to see them the following day. Then I went to Bess's house and told her of my plans.

She listened in silence and then got up and went to the window. "What's the matter, Bess? Look, if I get a job, I'll send for you. . . . I have to go. There's no work here." (Truthfully, though, I had the wanderlust in my soul.)

"I know that, Harry," she said quietly, turning to me. "It's . . . it's just that you seem so . . . well, *happy* about leaving."

I guess I was too excited to see the pain in her eyes. "Ah . . . Bess, this is a big chance for me, for *us!* Come on, Bess, give me a big smile!"

I suppose Bess knew me well enough by then to know it was no use to argue with me about anything, once my mind was made up. Stubborn was my middle name. We promised to write one another faithfully.

The next day I met the elderly couple. Their name was Hughes. He was a tall, dour fellow. Even when he told me I would do he didn't smile or shake my hand. Seems he was all business, and he was looking for someone who could not only drive, but help him sell his product, which was something called "the monkey ink pad."

He showed me a pencil with a rubber stamp on the end, where the eraser would ordinarily be. Pressing the stamp to an ink pad and then to a piece of paper, he made an imprint of a tiny monkey with a curly tail. He used the monkey stamp to show customers how the pad worked. It seemed easy enough, and it really was a good product.

A few days later we took off for California, stopping at banks and stores in towns along the way, to sell those funny monkey ink pads. I didn't make much money, hardly enough to pay my expenses.

Hughes was stingy with a dollar and was quick to criticize. When we finally got to California, we stayed with his sister and her husband in Los Angeles, while I sought work. About a week after we arrived, Hughes announced to me one night: "Hey, kid! You can't stay here anymore. I want you packed and out of here in the morning!" Just like that. Not that I wanted to stay, but he did it in such a cold, unfeeling way. I had outlived my usefulness. It was a harsh lesson I learned in the ways of human nature.

I hitchhiked my way down to San Diego, where I met up with an ex-carnival pitchman by the name of Gene Kipke. Gene was a personable guy, with blond hair, blue eyes, and a way with the women. We became buddies and teamed up in our travels.

Gene had a pocketful of fake diamonds called "white stones." We'd ask a restaurant owner if we could stand in front of his place and sell those stones to passersby, until we had enough for a meal. And if the owner said no, we would offer to wash dishes for a meal.

We worked our way in this fashion from San Diego to Galveston, Texas, where we arrived at the end of November 1935. Gene promptly split for Chicago, his hometown, and I went to look up Johnny Smith, a former high school fraternity brother who was living in Galveston.

Johnny, it turned out, had an excellent job with Todd-Galveston Dry Docks. He was glad to see me, but was taken aback by my threadbare appearance. I looked pretty seedy by that time. After feeding me, he put me up in a hotel for a few days.

One night, he took me out to his home to meet his family. After dinner he asked, "Harry, haven't you had enough? You know, there are thousands of guys just like you, crisscrossing the country, looking for work. Don't be so pigheaded and stubborn! Go home! Go back to Jersey, where you belong!"

"Maybe I will . . . soon as I earn enough money."

Reaching into his pocket, Johnny took out an envelope and pushed it toward me, almost shyly. "Harry, this is enough for a bus ticket and a little to eat on. Don't say anything. You can pay me back, after you get home and find a job."

I looked away, feeling ashamed of my need and touched by Johnny's generosity, his kindness. I knew he was right. Time to go home. . . .

Four days later, I alighted from the bus at the corner of Wall Street and Norwood Avenue in West Long Branch. I knew the fellow who owned the gas station there. He gave me a lift home. It was night.

Unbeknown to me, my folks had had a huge tree in our front yard cut down. The stump had just been removed, leaving a deep hole near the walk. Now, I had traveled thousands of miles without so much as stubbing my toe, but when I jumped down from the car with my bags, I stepped into that four-foot-deep hole and nearly broke my leg. I hadn't written my parents in some time, so they were totally unprepared and very shocked to see me, standing there in the door, disheveled and stained with dirt.

"That's a heck of a way to greet your long-lost son!" I cried with a grin, as my oldest sister ran to throw her arms around me. "Dig a hole in the yard so I can break my leg!"

Even before I cleaned up, I called Bess. I had missed her much more than I realized I would. It had been six long months. After supper I rushed right over to see her. We had a lot of catching up to do.

Bess hugged me and kissed me, then cried. Then she laughed and kissed me again—and then she *cried* again. It was great seeing her. I knew now I was deeply in love with Bess.

Things were still bad, but Bess got me a temporary sales job in the department store where she worked, just for the Christmas holidays. I knew that I wanted a solid job, making real money. So after the holidays, I went with an electrical appliance firm, the Scoby Company. I was given a drawing account of just $10 a week for four weeks. I was supposed to make the $10 back in commissions, and if I hadn't recouped the $40 by the end of the month, there was no more drawing account. That would be it!

I was selling refrigerators door to door. In the dead of winter in the Depression year of 1936, that was like selling snowballs to the Eskimos. While I was halfheartedly trying to sell, and failing, I noticed two well-dressed men who came into our showroom from time to time. They exuded confidence. They were salesmen, too, from Westinghouse and General Electric. They had good cars in which to travel about. I had no car. I walked all day, door to door, through the slush and snow. The image of those prosperous salesmen stuck in my mind.

If they can do it, so can I! I told myself. *I just haven't been trying hard enough!* That's when I really became a salesman. Through February and March my sales began to rise dramatically. *By April, I was leading the entire Eastern United States in sales for Westinghouse appliances.*

I was making money hand over fist. In an era when $25 a week was considered princely, I was pulling down $200! I began to buy nice clothes again. Next came a car. And I was able to take Bess to nice places for the first time. It's funny, no sparks had gone off when Bess and I first met, but I knew I was in love. Bess was, too, but was playing hard to get.

One night I asked her: "Bess, if you ever got an engagement ring from a fellow, what kind would you want?"

"I don't want an engagement ring from anybody," she replied coyly, looking at me.

"You *don't?*" I asked, feeling a sudden pang. "Well . . . *if* you wanted one, what kind would you like?"

Tossing her long black hair, she looked up at me and said airily, "Oh, I'd want a *big* diamond, a carat or more." I couldn't tell whether she was joking or serious.

"Uh . . . would you like gold or silver, or . . ."

"It would have to be set in 18-carat gold. No silver or platinum for me!"

That Christmas Eve, when we were all gathered at Bess's home, was the big night. Everyone had opened his presents at the stroke of midnight. Now, all eyes were on Bess.

"Bess, dear," her mother asked, "aren't you going to open the box Harry gave you before? You know, the little one—that one, just behind you."

Bess blushed. She had hidden the little box. She was afraid. She knew her mother didn't quite approve of me because I liked to drink and was known as something of a "hell raiser" around town.

"Do . . . do I *have* to?" Bess asked unhappily, feeling behind her for the tiny box. Then, with trembling fingers she tore the paper off, opened it, and held it up.

"Oh . . . Harry, I love it!" she cried softly, staring at the ring. Going over to examine it, her mother exclaimed, "Harry, I really do like it much better in the gold than I did the platinum!"

"You knew all about it!" Bess sputtered, turning beet red.

"All I can say is it's about time!" her dad quipped. Everyone roared with delight.

A few days later, Bess's father asked her, "Don't you have a right hand anymore?" She had been waving her left hand under the noses of her family, friends, and every shop clerk in West Long Branch.

But her father was adamant about me getting what he called a "steady job" before he would allow us to marry. It didn't matter that I was earning hundreds of dollars a week. "Working on a commission basis is not a regular, steady job," he declared. "You're doing just fine now, Harry, but how *steady* is it?"

So, reluctantly I took a job (arranged, naturally, through Bess's uncle) with the Bankers Commercial Security Corporation in New York, at the munificent salary of $25 a week.

Bess and I were married in a small church ceremony in September 1938.

We rented a little house, in Oakhurst, New Jersey, in the shore area. We could have bought the place for the then outrageous sum of $3,300, but we thought it excessive when you had to go outside to get into the cellar! We were holding out for something better.

I honestly tried to like my "steady" job, but it was rough. I was called an adjuster, which really meant that I was a "loan ranger"; I repossessed automobiles in and around the Amboys, which was populated predominantly with immigrants in those days.

People tend to get emotional when you try to take back their cars, regardless of the fact that they can't pay for them. I felt I could handle myself, but several times excited men actually pulled shotguns and threatened me. I tried to be fair about things, and seemed to have a knack for calming the wildest of my "clients."

Eventually, the company promoted me to Unit Manager and moved me to their headquarters on Madison Avenue in Manhattan. I guess I was on my way up the corporate ladder.

Dutifully I commuted to New York City daily for about a year. But I was extremely unhappy. Everybody on those trains looked alike—pinstriped suits, attaché cases and newspapers. I felt like a big penguin, in a flock of penguins.

It was stifling. I was an adventurer, a wanderer—no, *more* than that: I was a born *maverick.*

Webster defines a maverick as "an unbranded range animal" and "an independent individual who refuses to conform with his group." That was me, all right. I knew I could never remain as part of the herd, going tamely to and from work on a nine-to-five basis. I'd go crazy if I had to do that for the rest of my life. I knew that for a fact.

Bess and I were on the beach one Sunday, when a friend asked me where he could find a "new businessman." He said he was opening an automobile finance company in Red Bank, less than a mile from my home, and he needed a man to solicit business from the local automobile agencies.

"How about me?" I asked.

"What! Are you crazy? You're with an excellent firm, Harry! You have a *good job!"* he retorted.

I persisted. "What can you do for me?"

"Well . . ." he said, "I can only pay you your present salary for one month—I can't afford any more."

"I'll take it!" I said.

Then I walked over to where Bess was sunning herself and told her what I had just done.

She looked away for a moment, out to the sea. Then she looked back at me. "Harry," she said, "you're the one who has to work and make the living for us. *You're* the one who has to put the food on the table. As long as you're happy at what you're doing, so am I.

"I don't care what business you go into, Har—just as long as it's honest."

Of course, when they heard, Bess's parents were unhappy—to put it mildly. I had quit a promising, steady job to take another that offered me nothing beyond a month's pay. But whatever they thought, they never mentioned it to me.

They needn't have been afraid. I did well at the new job. In fact, I brought in so much business, that at the end of the first month I was made a partner. I felt I was well on my way. Ten years of this and I would have it made.

But I was establishing a pattern. I would work at a job just as long as it was a challenge; when it settled into a routine, I'd quit without fear or hesitation. There was always money to be made selling, and I felt I could sell. People seemed to like me. Most important, I never doubted I would succeed.

In December 1941, World War II erupted. The bands playing and the flags flying made me feel patriotic. After three years of marriage, Bess and I still hadn't been able to have children, so early in 1942 we agreed that I would enlist and do my bit. We had enough money in the bank, and we agreed that Bess would return to her parents' home while I was away. I chose the army.

For me it was a whole new adventure, a new challenge. I never doubted that I would survive the war and come back to Bess. I always seemed to come out of things on my feet.

The war was over quickly for me. I sustained a severe shoulder injury playing war games at A.P. Hill in Virginia. In the next months I passed through a series of army hospitals, finally being discharged from the army through Woodrow Wilson General in Staunton, Virginia.

I returned home—a disabled veteran who had never fired a shot, never engaged the enemy. My dream of adventure and fighting and subsequent glory had been ended by a stupid accident. Of course, I never stopped to consider that had I gone overseas with my unit, I might have been killed. That never entered my mind for one moment.

Bess was happy to have me home alive and in one piece, even though I was permanently damaged goods. I was still recuperating and unable to work. I couldn't handle that. It made me mad at the world.

A few years earlier, Bess's Aunt Louise had nearly died of a cerebral hemorrhage and complications. They told the family that if she ever got through the crisis, she'd be a cabbage. Aunt Louise was a Christian Scientist, so Bess's father called in her practitioner. Within a week or so, Aunt Louise was up and about, and a short time later she went out and got a job!

Bess was very impressed by this, so she began reading some of the Christian Science literature Aunt Louise sent. We both did. Bess thought there might be something to it, though the practice of not going to medical doctors at all seemed a bit extreme to her.

The religion part of Christian Science left me rather cold, as did all religion. But the idea of using the latent power of the mind—of thinking positively—to bring about healing, intrigued me. But that's all it was at the time, an interesting idea. I soon forgot about it.

Now that I was disabled, I could have used some positive thinking. Instead, I was overwhelmed by self-pity and anger. It was my first real defeat. I began to drink.

Previously, I used to enjoy "tieing one on" with the boys, once in a while. But now I was hanging out in bars and drinking every night. Our formerly fat bank account was dwindling rapidly. I really didn't seem to care—about anything.

At first, Bess tried to be understanding. After all, I had suffered a terrific injury to my ego as well as my body. But as months went by and my drinking continued unabated, she became apprehensive, and then alarmed.

One night, after I had come home from the bar, Bess confronted me. "Harry, listen to me!" Her voice was hard, shrill. *Why was she so mad?* I wondered.

"Harry, I'm pregnant! We're going to have a baby!"

"Oh, Hon . . . that's great! Finally . . . a baby!"

"Harry, either you stop drinking, *now,* or I'm going to leave you! I mean it! Harry, I love you, but my baby is not going to have a drunkard for a father! Do you understand me?"

I nodded my head slowly. I had never seen Bess like this before. She meant business. I was crushed with guilt.

My drinking stopped. Not all at once, but gradually. I *had* to stop—I didn't want to lose Bess; and I was going to be a father! More than anything else, I think that is what enabled me to get myself straightened out. It enabled me to stop feeling sorry for myself, to stop being mad at the world. *Me, a father!* How about that? I had always wanted a little curly-haired girl. (I was sure it would be a girl!)

Before the baby was born, I managed to scrape enough money together to start my own insurance agency, selling fire coverage to homeowners and small businessmen. I knew a lot of people in town and I did fairly well.

After a few months I was offered a substantial job with a big firm. Because the baby was coming, I felt I had better take the job. General Adjustment Bureau was a national concern. They took me on as an insurance adjuster, at considerably more than I was making on my own, plus expenses. It was the one time I sacrificed my independence for security. I sold my business and went with them. I worked for them for the next six years.

In the course of events, a hurricane struck Florida in 1949. I was sent down, with an army of other insurance adjusters, all marshalled by General Adjustment Bureau and drawn from all over the country.

When disaster strikes the homes and belongings of people, they react in different ways. Some are greedy, some are very honest, and some are *almost* honest. I found the poorer the people, the more honest they were.

You will never be nearer to a man than when you are adjusting his insurance claim. You are dealing with his pocketbook. These people will always remember you, because they've just been hit with what may be the biggest crisis of their lives, and you were there, as their salvation and their money man.

The insurance adjuster, however, holds the whip hand over the person who has a claim from a storm, fire or flood; and many adjusters exercise their power ruthlessly and arbitrarily. I was never that way. To me, insurance adjusting meant just that—*adjusting*. It didn't mean being adamant or arbitrary with these poor people.

Of course, over the years, no matter how many disasters I dealt with, no matter how many stunned faces I saw, none of it had anything to do with me *personally*. Disaster was just my job; a job I tried to do fairly, but a job, nevertheless. Disaster might touch others—smash their hopes and dreams, their very lives—but it never occurred to me for one second that any such thing could ever happen to Harry De-Camp. Not even remotely.

On August 23, 1944, after almost six childless years, Bess delivered a beautiful little baby girl. We named her Judy. Not Judith—a fact to which her teachers were never to concede—but *Judy*. Judy is a cute name, and she was a cute baby, with a delightful smile and a halo of dark, curly hair. I was a doting daddy, a proud daddy, the proudest daddy in the world. She was just what I always wanted!

Judy turned out to be like me—mental in her approach to life (whereas her mother tends to be emotional and intuitive about things).

When she was a toddler, Bess began to take her to Sunday school, which was all right with me; but she never enrolled her in any. At this point I suppose Bess wasn't sure which was the *right* religion any more—and this from a woman who had taught Sunday school in the Methodist church as a girl. It was probably the result of living with me all those years.

She said she intended to expose Judy to all religions so she could make up her own mind when she was of age. She even took her to Christian Science Sunday school for a while. I had no more than a passing interest in any of them.

Still, I liked Bess's approach. I always encouraged Judy to think for herself. When she got to school and would come to me with a question, whether it was about God or earthquakes or boys, instead of giving her the answer, I would ask her to sit down and tell me what *she* thought about it.

To me, the worst thing was to accept something, and believe it, just because somebody in authority said it was so. You had to learn to think for yourself. Too many people are going around with braces on their brains.

As Judy was growing up, I'd have friends over on a Saturday night, and we'd get to talking. We would have a good time, discussing everything from politics to flying saucers. I would argue one point of view, making it sound totally valid. Then, when I had everyone agreeing with me, I'd take the opposite view and would demolish the arguments I had just constructed. It was fun.

Judy would eavesdrop and was fascinated by these sessions, soaking it all up. I prided myself on being a rationalist, and I communicated this to Judy.

When we weren't talking, we'd often play baseball in the evenings. It's a hard, competitive world. I encouraged her never to be a quitter—in sports, in her studies, in anything. The older Judy got, the closer we drew together. Bess used to ask me in those days, "Harry, if we had another child, would you have wanted a boy?"

"Never," I'd reply. "I'll take a girl every time. Boys go down to the corner, but girls stay at home with their fathers."

Bess was a good wife and homemaker. In that era before Women's Liberation, she did more than bake and clean and sew dresses for Judy. In 1950, when we decided to begin building our own home, Bess not only planned it; she actually drew up the blueprints! (They were so professionally executed that the architect signed them!)

Our home was going to be a beautiful little ranch-style house, modern and all on one level, with plenty of property around it.

Just about then, I had an argument with my boss at General Adjustment Bureau, and we parted company, just as the shell of our dream home was being erected on that nice piece of property on Hendrickson Place.

I left on November 1, 1950, with only two weeks severence. But I guess somebody up there must have liked me (though I didn't give Him credit), because on November 25, a hurricane hit the East Coast. The whole Jersey shore area was in a shambles, with millions of dollars in damage—and insurance claims.

Two days after the storm, I got a call from the Hartford Insurance Company, asking if I was interested in handling claims. I said no, but after some prodding, agreed to do it temporarily. I didn't even have paper, so I took down the names of the first claimants on brown paper bags.

The next day, Maryland Casualty Insurance Company was on the phone with the same deal, and then Glens Falls and Aetna called. Within a week I had a load of files all over my living room floor! I enlisted Bess's help, and my sister-in-law's, and then had to hire a girl.

The "temporary job," as it turned out, lasted fifteen years. The work just never stopped rolling in. Best of all, I was in business as an independent adjuster, for the insurance companies. Again I was on my own—and I loved it.

In 1965, I decided that the adjusting business was too tiring for a man approaching 55, so I bought an insurance agency. Then, in 1969, I went into partnership with a friend, Tony Camassa, so we were DeCamp-Camassa Associates. Our company was housed in a beautiful shingled building on Oceanport Avenue in West Long Branch. It's still there.

I had gotten into local politics prior to purchasing the insurance agency. Starting in the early 1950s, among other things, I had been director of Civil Defense for West Long Branch, a member of the zoning board for five years (three as president), a member of the borough council for two years, and served two years on the New Jersey State Commission on Aging.

Our agency thrived and over the years I became a charter member of all the civic organizations in town. I loved it all. I was (and am) particularly proud that I founded and served as the first president of our local Chamber of Commerce. But my favorite honor was becoming a charter member of the West Long Branch Lions Club.

In 1964, Judy's college education was cut short by a near-fatal automobile accident, which left Bess and I shaken. After a long, slow recovery, our daughter met and fell in love with Rick Riggenbach, a personable young man I already knew through the Long Branch Ice Boat and Yacht Club.

It was a big, old-fashioned church wedding. Bess cried, as I proudly walked down the aisle and gave my lovely Judy to Rick in marriage.

By now, DeCamp-Camassa had grown to a point where I could take my son-in-law into the firm. I had finally arrived at a period in my life where I could afford to take some long dreamt-of trips: three to Europe and one to Hawaii. My wanderlust seemed satisfied at last.

During all those years of working, changing jobs, getting involved in politics and civic groups, and raising a family, I was full of energy. Except for my World War II injury, I don't think I ever had a sick day in my older life. Which is why the news that I was now suffering from—for crying out loud—*cancer,* was such a blow. I found it hard to accept, even to *comprehend.*

That first interminably long night, knowing I had cancer, dragged on. I lay in that semi-darkened room, pondering my past life. It had been a full, exciting life, but in many ways, an ordinary one. I guessed that, after all, I was just an ordinary guy. An average Joe.

I had made my own mark; I had contributed to my profession and my community. I had a lovely wife and daughter. And that was something. The seeds of my posterity, my immortality (the only one in which I believed) were in my two beautiful granddaughters, Holly and Heidi. Sixty-six years, gone by so fast . . . so fast.

And what of the future? Was it possible that I would now *die* in the same hospital where I had been born, all those long years ago? The irony was cruel. I was fairly big physically—six foot two and 235 pounds. Cynically I wondered if

I would break any records for size going out of this world, as I had when I came into it.

I would have to talk seriously to my son-in-law Rick. I'd sell him my interest in the firm. I would have to retire now, of course. Me retire? What on earth would I do with myself with the time I had left?

Hold on there, Harry! I chided myself again. *It's only bladder cancer, remember? That isn't so serious. Hundreds of people have had bladder cancer and lived.* They could clean it up without much trouble. I wasn't *really* sick, at least not like Vince and my two friends. Poor guys! I decided that the next morning I would look in on them. Only this time I would be in bathrobe and slippers. There was something a bit comical about that. With these thoughts fading in and out, I finally drifted off to sleep.

3

The White Light

"Therefore I have hewn them by the prophets, I have slain them by the words of my mouth, and my judgment goes forth as the light."

Hosea 6:5 RSV

The next morning my morbid thoughts had vanished with the sun. I was my old self again. The next two days were fairly routine. I did visit Vince and my two friends. As always, I commiserated with them, joked with them, even felt sorry for them. It still didn't occur to me to feel sorry for myself, because I still couldn't accept the fact that there was anything too seriously wrong with me—at least not anything the doctors couldn't cure.

The following weekend I was released from Monmouth Medical Center, and on Monday I returned to the office and my normal work routine. However, the thought of retirement kept nagging me. I was sixty-six, after all. Maybe I should call it quits. . . .

I sat down with Rick and seriously discussed his purchasing my share of DeCamp-Camassa. In a few weeks the details were worked out and the deal was consummated to the satisfaction of all parties concerned.

There was the inevitable series of small retirement parties. I heard all the usual well-meant clichéd farewells: "We'll miss you, boss. . . ." "There'll never be another like you. . . ." "They broke the mold after they made you, Har." "Come back and see us, hear!" Yet the undertone, the unspoken word, was obvious—*"Good old Harry won't be with us much longer . . . has cancer, you know. . . ."*

I accepted the accolades and farewells with mixed emotions. "What do you think, Bess? Do they mean all those nice things they're saying?"

"Oh, Hon, I'm certain they really mean them," soothed Bess.

The radiology department at Monmouth Medical contacted me, asking me to come in at my earliest convenience. I dropped by and met with the chief radiologist. Sitting in his office, he laid out the plan of attack on my cancer. He assured me that my doctor had been fully briefed and had agreed to the procedure.

"Harry," the radiologist began, "we'll measure the location of the cancer, then determine the depth to which we must penetrate—and the required time exposure. Then we'll draw a schematic on you with indelible ink, to mark the exact location.

"Now you're not to take a shower or bath until this treatment is over. Stand-up sponge baths, yes—but nothing else. Understand?"

"Yes," I acknowledged. "How long will these treatments last? And what are they—cobalt? X ray?"

"X ray. They'll be given to you every day, five days a week, for eight weeks."

Eight weeks! I thought, sucking in my breath. "Then what happens?" I asked.

"We check you periodically. From then on, there will be no further expense to you," he added with a slight smile.

"When do I start these treatments?"

"Let's see," he said, checking his calendar. "Today is Thursday . . . next Monday. We have to fit you into a time slot that will be your time exclusively until the day the treatments end. The time will be . . . ah, let's see . . . 1:15 P.M. okay?"

I nodded in agreement, but I had that scared feeling a kid feels on the first day of school.

"Fine!" he said cheerfully, standing up. "See you Monday!"

At one o'clock on Monday, Bess and I entered the radiology waiting room. I shall never forget it.

What am I doing here? I thought. *What a sorry group! This is for sick people . . . not me . . . I'm not sick!* I wondered if I looked like those people. *No . . . I couldn't . . . I just couldn't!*

"Do I, Bess? Do I look like *them?*" I whispered frantically.

"No. Hon, you look like a visitor," she assured me.

In that room were old people, young people, little children, bloated people, emaciated people, people on bed carts, people in wheelchairs, people weeping, people moaning, people talking, some of them talking to no one in particular; staring straight ahead with blank eyes.

They didn't seem to be people at all; they were animated bodies. They reminded me of a TV movie I once saw about zombies. Here they were: the living dead!

All the bodies were marked with indelible schematic maps—some on the throat, some on the face, some on shaved heads, some on the upper arm—and some like me, on their bellies. (We were the lucky ones; our clothing covered the bizarre markings.)

The painted zombies either shuffled about or sat silently awaiting their turns. I knew they were secretly hoping against hope that these treatments would cure their dreaded cancer. You could see it in their eyes. But the feeling that pervaded that room was not hope, but utter *hopelessness.* You could actually feel it.

I can't face this, day after day! I thought.

But I did. Each day for the next eight weeks I waited with the zombies. At 1:15 I would be called from that sorry human mass to be ushered into a large room for my treatment.

The walls of this room were concrete, several feet thick. The glass picture windows were also very thick. It reminded me of a World War II bunker. To enter or leave the room, you had to zigzag around corners to find the single massive metal door.

The room was bare except for two objects. The first of these was a long narrow table on wheels. The tabletop was made up of movable sections that could be placed into any desired sequence. One of these sections was of heavy Plexiglas.

On the far side of the room was a huge iron "monster" which rose toward the ceiling from a heavy-soled, semicircular base, then jutted out into the middle of the room at a 90-degree angle. At the end of the monster was a huge glaring "eye" that stared down at the table.

The table sections were aligned by an attendant so that the Plexiglas block was under my buttocks. My pelvic area would then be bared, the "eye" focusing on the schematic.

"Ready, Mr. DeCamp?" a disembodied voice would ask from an intercom, after the attendants had scurried away.

Then directions would follow directions, and the huge monster would hum and then clang into action. The eye would swing around, scanning my body, shooting invisible shafts into me from one angle, then another. This would go on for about eight to ten minutes.

Then the command: "All done. Please dress and report to the front desk."

After the treatment, I would await the doctor of the day who would push his hands into my bladder, my stomach, my arm pits, and would then feel the glands of my neck. "Okay, Harry—see you tomorrow."

This procedure was repeated five days a week for eight long weeks. (Actually it was nine weeks, because the "monster" broke down and one extra week was added.)

As the treatments progressed, the invisible X rays had their inevitable effect: my bladder became spasmatic. The spasms became progressively worse; the last two weeks were pure hell. They would occur as I tried to urinate. The feeling was awful, like a fist slowly clenching, until the pressure and pain were unbearable. I would grab onto whatever was near—a sink, a cabinet, anything—and hold tight, grimacing like a crazy man until the spasm passed. Then my bladder would empty. I actually dreaded having to go to the bathroom, something that heretofore I had taken for granted.

In addition to the X-ray therapy, every three months I dutifully returned to the hospital for three days to have the spots on my bladder cauterized. This went on for twenty months.

During this time, my brother-in-law Vince was going downhill very fast. So were my two friends, Mel and George. One day, after I had returned from the operating room during one of those every-three-month procedures, Dr. Demaree, our family physician dropped in, just as I was getting everything back into focus.

"How do you feel, big fellow?" he inquired.

"Just fine, but a little groggy right now," I replied.

"You sure?"

"Yes," I countered. "I'm just fine . . . sleepy, but fine."

"Harry, we lost Vince this morning, while you were in the operating room. I'm . . . I'm sorry."

I remained silent for a long time. We had expected it, but Vince . . . gone! The doctor patted my shoulder and left the room.

Vince and I had been good friends as well as brothers-in-law. We had learned to fly together; we were both World War II veterans; both of us were interested in photography (though jokingly we used to admit that neither of us was very good at it). We had even lived across the street from each other, so the family ties were pretty close. It was hard to envision Vince gone. I felt as though a rock had been placed squarely on my chest. I knew it would feel lighter if I could cry, but somehow I couldn't.

* * *

The following day I was released from the hospital at noon. Bess picked me up. She looked terrible. "Hon," she said, "I'm so sick to my stomach with a virus . . . I can't go to the funeral parlor to help Aud." (Audrey, Bess's sister, was Vince's widow.) "I'll be lucky to make it home," Bess fairly gasped.

"Honey, I'll go and help Aud," I volunteered.

"Harry, can you handle it?" she said, her brow furrowed with concern. "Are you strong enough? Do you feel well enough?"

"I'm fit as a fiddle!" I lied.

I spent two afternoons and evenings at the funeral parlor, comforting Audrey and visiting with family friends.

People were startled—astounded really—to see me at the bier, looking healthy, greeting them with Aud. Some of them would actually hesitate to shake my hand; others would pull their hands away, a bit too quickly. *These people are mistaken,* I thought, *I'm going to live.*

It's something how people act around a cancer patient, particularly at funerals. Someone actually said to Bess, "Isn't it a shame that Harry's got cancer. How long do you suppose he's got?" Never mind Bess's feelings, I was standing right next to her when it was said! The person acted as though I weren't even there.

"People are really strange," I remarked to Bess. "They either act like I'm going to give them something, or they look like they expect me to drop dead any minute."

I never once connected Vince's cancer, or his death, to my situation. Nor did Bess for that matter. Vince had a melanoma—a cancer that begins from a black mole. Vince was a Swede and for some reason, a disproportionate number of blue-eyed blonds fall victim to this kind of tumor. We understood it was a much more serious form of cancer than my bladder type.

The funeral was the third day. The whole thing was very tiring and trying, but I did it. Looking back on it, I feel a curious sense of satisfaction that I managed to rise to the occasion, to forget my own problems and think of my poor sister-in-law. I still wear the memory of that time like a badge of honor, though I don't consider myself an overly prideful man.

Then, within months, Mel and George died. With a saddened heart I attended both funerals. My emotions ran rampant. Sometimes I cried for no apparent reason. Sometimes I became enraged at the very thought of cancer. At other times I became fearful that I would be joining Vince, Mel, and George as the fourth! These morbid thoughts and feelings would pass, though, and I would feel just fine. Yet even in my most optimistic, tranquil moments I was waiting for the second shoe to hit the floor . . . waiting . . . *waiting.*

During one of my three-day visits to the hospital, in September 1977, I had a very traumatic experience. It was to be the first of two such incidents.

I was "prepped" and wheeled into the operating room to have the cancer spots burned out. Just before I was put to sleep I jokingly said to him, "Doctor, if you keep on with these 'burn' jobs, they'll nickname you, 'The Torch.' " He just laughed. His smiling face was the last thing I saw before the sodium pentothal knocked me out.

During the routine procedure of examining the inside of my bladder with a cystoscope and the burning of the cancer spots, something went wrong. To this day, no one has told me exactly what it was.

Usually during the cauterization procedure I would go "out," experiencing nothing but blankness until I came to. But this time, after I blacked out, I became conscious on another level. I was aware that I was up against "something" on my left. It may have been a wall, or my physical body—I don't really know what it was; it's hard to explain.

At any rate, I next moved or slid away from whatever "it" was, horizontally, like a letter slipping out of an envelope.

I was in total darkness—I mean, *pitch blackness.* I felt terribly alone in that black void. And I was conscious all the time and aware that I was conscious. It was as if I were there in my mind and body, yet I knew instinctively that I was in another world, or dimension. It was frightening.

Off to my right was a broken skyline of some kind . . . buildings. Over this skyline and silhouetting it was a big ball of white light. The light was brilliant, *brilliant.*

I floated in a prone position out into the black void, drifting toward that brilliant white light over the skyline. It wasn't a "good" light or a "bad" light. It was simply a shining light, *but for some reason I feared it.*

"No!" I screamed. "I can't go now!" My mind raced . . . *I didn't make it. I'm dead!* Then the thought hit me again with a sickening reality: *I'M DEAD!*

I screamed again into that vast darkness: "I *can't* go! I have too much to do yet! Help! Help me . . . someone! Help . . . !" (They told me later that I was actually screaming aloud.)

It was a terrible feeling, knowing I was alone, thinking I was never, ever going back into the world of the living. It was horrible—just stark fear!

Then, quite suddenly I stopped moving up into that mysterious white light. I remained, hovering there for a few minutes, and I could hear my heart begin to pound. Then, slowly, I slid downhill to my left, meeting whatever it was I had left and fitting into it.

"Hold on, Harry!" a man's voice was shouting in my left ear. "Hold on, Harry! Fight it! Don't let go!"

It was the doctor's voice. I knew it was him, because he has an accent. There was no mistaking that.

I was now conscious of the nurse holding me under my right arm and the doctor holding my left.

"Mr. DeCamp, come back!" screamed a woman's voice in my right ear. The plea was shouted over and over: "Come back!"

Then I was being pulled around and pummelled and there were sounds of a commotion. "Work on him! Work on him! Get his eyes open!"

My eyelids fluttered. I could see my doctor, his face, anxious and perspiring, staring into my own. Behind him the nurse was staring down at me, wide-eyed.

It was a terrifying experience. I have never been quite that scared in my life. And, having survived to tell about it, I shall never, ever forget it.

I was scared for days and weeks after this strange experience. I told Bess that I knew that when you die you go *somewhere,* because I had been there. And then I'd start to cry. I was so upset about it that I'd cry for no reason at all.

"Har," Bess would ask me, "was it a good experience or bad?" And I'd think a minute then reply, "I'm . . . I'm not sure . . . but it was more like bad than good. . . . It was so . . . lonely there."

I dreamed about it at night and would come awake with a start, my pajamas soaked through with sweat.

I questioned the doctor about it. "Harry," he would say, "you're very emotional, very emotional." That was all. He wouldn't look me in the eye, and he would almost scurry away each time I asked the blunt question that I knew was true: *"I died on that table, didn't I?"*

4

The "Bag"

"Such are the paths of all who forget God . . . His confidence breaks in sunder, and his trust is a spider's web. He leans against his house, but it does not stand; He lays hold of it, but it does not endure."

Job 8:13–15 RSV

Bess and I lived through weeks of trauma resulting from that really terrifying "out of the body" experience. Maybe I'm wrong, but that's the only way I can describe it. I had to try to figure out what it was myself, because neither my doctor, nor anyone else for that matter, would ever confirm or deny that anything at all unusual had happened during that supposedly routine procedure.

Since then, I've read articles about other people having such strange experiences during surgery—some of these "visions" are far more detailed than mine, but I doubt that any was more frightening. The vast majority of accounts of the "near-death" or "out of the body" experience describe a beatific meeting with a wonderful Being of Light, whom many identify as Christ. In the presence of this Being, they know feelings of ineffable serenity, joy, and fulfillment. Many do not want to come back to the physical world, which ever after seems joyless and dull by comparison. For most, the fear of death vanishes.

I have asked myself why I experienced just the opposite feelings. Why did I feel such total, abject terror in that black void, as I moved up into that brilliant white light? Now, almost five years later, I believe that it was a real experience and not a drug-induced hallucination. I *knew* I was dead, and I feared death, because I was not ready to go.

Of course, during those weeks that followed, this never consciously entered my mind. At the time I was an irreligious man, one who gave intellectual assent to the idea of God without ever seriously having more than a nodding acquaintance with Him. In that black void, the fact that I was a "good" husband and family man and a sociable fellow gave me no comfort at all. I think now that I was on my way to meet my Maker, and *I wasn't ready.* That was what struck terror into my heart.

Ironically, though I told Bess that I knew that a man goes somewhere when he dies, because it had happened to me, it never once occurred to me to investigate what that "somewhere" might be and why it frightened me. I might have found out by opening the nearest Bible. But such is the spiritual blindness of the "natural" unregenerate man.

While I was recovering from my terror, I had other serious things to consider. When the doctor examined me during that fateful procedure, he suspected something was going on behind the bladder. The only way to find out was to "go inside" and take a look. Exploratory surgery was scheduled for February 1978.

All through Christmas and New Year's I worried and sweated about the impending surgery. I tried to keep my mind off it, but it was no use. For Bess and me the holidays were like flat champagne; the body was there but the sparkle we had enjoyed every year at Christmas was gone.

The awful possibility that hung over the holiday festivities like a pall was that my bladder might be removed during the operation. In a sobering conference with Bess and me, the doctor had spelled it out—depending on the extent to which the bladder itself was involved in the spread of the malignancy, he might or might not elect to remove it. He asked for our permission to do so.

"Don't worry about it, Harry," he said, "having a bag for a bladder isn't the worst thing in the world." And he added, trying to sound casual about it, "Many people live very normal lives without a bladder, and so can you, if necessary."

My mind rebelled at the thought that I might have to spend the rest of my life without a bladder. It was soul-crushing. I couldn't bear the thought that the body that had served me so well all my life would be changed by the surgeon's knife. I would be condemned to wear one of those awful bags for the rest of my days. There would be a hole in my side with a tube coming out of it! Could I wear a belt for my pants? Would the bag fall off at inappropriate times? How do you empty one gracefully, and how do you know *when?*

I'd be a freak. Would Bess accept it? Would she even want me in bed beside her? All these thoughts kept churning inside me until one night I exploded: "I don't want to have the damned bladder out!"

Sitting close beside me, Bess said, "Harry, if you have to have it out, you have to have it out. *There is nothing you can do about it.*" She laid out the words slowly and forcefully, so the idea would finally sink in.

"It'll be awful for you to put up with!" I spat out, pulling my hands away, as if I already had that bag attached to my side.

"Oh . . . Harry!" Bess said, taking my face in her hands. "If it comes to that. . . . Listen to me good; I've loved you all these years. It's been a wonderful marriage. Physical love is a part of that, but as important as it is, it isn't marriage itself. Don't you see, Honey? Marriage is living every day, sharing our problems, working them out together, caring for each other—trying to do the best we can!"

I looked away, because my eyes had filled. I was feeling sorry for myself, sorry for Bess, sorry about the years that were gone, the happy, *healthy* years. . . .

"You know, Har," she continued, "the women were discussing breast cancer a few weeks ago at the ceramic club meeting, and one of them said, 'Oh, I wouldn't dare let them do a mastectomy on me! Why my husband wouldn't stay married to me!' I just looked at her and said, 'Any man who would love me just for *that,* well . . . he can go to the devil!' Boy, did that burn me up!

"Do you understand what I'm trying to say, Harry? It's *you* I love, the person inside . . . for better or worse. So let's not worry about how awful it will be for me."

My true blue, wonderful Bess. To her, life was just too fundamental, too basic, to let a little thing like a bag faze her. We'd accept it and just get on with living. That talk helped me tremendously. It made the prospect of wearing a bag almost bearable. Once I accepted that possibility, I wanted to get the whole thing over with as quickly as possible. Now it was the waiting that was upsetting me more than anything.

Finally February first arrived, raw and blustery; I reentered Monmouth Medical Center. Again I went through the routine that hospitals require of anyone seeking admittance to the sacred and expensive precincts. I couldn't help but wonder why they hadn't gotten my mother's maiden name the first time around. . . .

I was put in a room on the fifth floor. The shades were drawn so the room was only dimly lit. I was aware of someone in the other bed, but I couldn't make out what he looked like. It turned out to be a fourteen-year-old boy, with cancer.

The poor kid had one of those awful tracheotomy holes in his neck, with a tube stuck in it. He appeared to be either asleep or in a semi-coma. At any rate, he didn't acknowledge me, nor did I acknowledge him. Yet I somehow felt he knew I was there, even though his eyes were closed.

Our room was opposite the nurse's station. It was arranged this way so the nurses could better keep an eye on the boy. They were compassionate and mothered him. That first day they whispered to me, "Mr. DeCamp, don't be offended when he explodes into a cursing rage." Looking at him lying in the semidarkness, pale and still, I couldn't imagine him raging. Still, I could certainly relate to it—having cancer at 14!

The boy's parents came in soon after I had settled in. They stood by his bed for a while. The woman smoothed back the damp hair from his brow, and talked quietly to him. The father stood awkwardly by, just staring at his wife and son.

They introduced themselves and told me their son had cancer. "He's terminal," the father said, without batting an eye. Then they started talking about the son's condition. It surprised me that they were so blatant. Obviously it was something to which they had long ago reconciled themselves. Seeing my almost startled reaction, the mother said with a sigh, "No . . . he can't hear us, Mr. DeCamp. Our son is . . . out of this world."

The very fact that they had a need to tell me, a total stranger, the most intimate facts of their son's illness, betrayed their deep pain. How my heart went out to them, as I lay there, listening to the dismal, almost compulsive recital! I supposed this was the thousandth time they had told it; to friends, relatives, strangers—anyone who would listen. I'm sure if I had been blind and deaf, they would have sat there talking.

Later that night, when all was still and just the boy and I were in the room, I heard him moaning and moving in bed. I spoke to him very softly. "Son . . . ? Can you hear me?" The groaning and the movement stopped immediately. He was conscious and he had heard me! But he said nothing. I supposed he could hear and understand, but couldn't speak. I wondered if he had heard and understood his parents talking earlier about his condition.

For the rest of the night he was quiet, except for the occasional rustle of sheets, which told me that at least he was still alive. It was not a good night for me, however. I was really upset about this kid.

When Bess arrived the next day, I promptly took her out into the hall and explained the circumstances to her. When we reentered the room, I was surprised to see the boy's large, dark eyes focused on us. Bess spoke softly to him, but he showed no recognition, no sign that he understood. He just stared at us.

Still, his dark eyes followed our every move. So, as we talked, we let drop in our conversation about how he would be sure to recover his health, how he would be returning to school and his friends, and how, someday he would look back on this as a youthful experience. Now we knew he was listening; we could see it in his eyes. It was heartrending.

That afternoon when my doctor came in and saw how upset I was, he got the picture immediately. "What are you doing here?" he fairly barked. "You should never have been put in here! We'll get you out, right now!"

He started to hurry from the room, then turning back to me he scolded, "Harry, you need to rest, physically and mentally, for your *own* operation! I want you ready for that. You have to worry about yourself! Do you understand me?"

I wanted to tell him that I didn't mind, that I thought I might be able to help the boy, somehow. But I knew it wouldn't do any good. Within minutes, I was at the other end of the hall.

I have never forgotten that boy. I spent time, later, tracing him down and was extremely happy to learn that he actually did recover! He was a senior in high school and was doing all the things a normal teenager would do. God is so wonderful, when we give Him a chance to work!

My new room was light and airy, with a view of the ocean off in the distance, half a mile away.

My roommate was about fifteen years younger than me. He was a pipefitter by trade, a rough-and-ready guy. But like many working men, he had a soft underside to his crusty exterior. We got along famously, and both Bess and I enjoyed visiting with his wife and entire family.

His name was Mickey, and he was in for a relatively minor problem. Mickey kept me entertained with his stories during the long, dull, anxious days and nights. He knew I had cancer, and he was solicitous and kind, in his gruff way. He was irrepressible; he bounced around the room and hallways like a rubber ball, his split-back hospital gown flying about his bare *derriere* like a sheet drying in the wind.

Mickey had an insatiable appetite for hot dogs. He would order his quota of two from the menu. Then, when his daughter came visiting, he would send her downstairs to the street-corner vendor for three or four more! Mickey would eat them all with gusto. Then he would lie there patting his stomach and proclaim to the world that "there's nothing as good as 'those dirty waters' from the pushcart vendors."

Mickey's antics and moral support kept me from concentrating on "the bag." Meanwhile, they were trying to prepare me for it, psychologically and physically.

The day before the operation a young man came in to see me. He began by announcing that he was wearing a bag and he showed it to me. "Mr. DeCamp," he said brightly, "I'm a bag wearer and I want to tell you how simple life can be for us." He then proceeded to explain the idiosyncrasies of "the bag" to me.

At first I was annoyed by the thought of having to consider a bag, but by the time he finished, I was saying, "It really isn't so bad, is it?"

He smiled and replied, "No, it isn't."

Knowledge sometimes has the power to lessen our fears. I really did feel relieved after that young man's visit. Yet, my sleep that night was fitful. About 4 A.M., after I had finally drifted off, a huge nurse waked me to take my blood pressure. Now, my history is dotted with people who have startled me, or awakened me suddenly—to their utter surprise. When that nurse startled me awake, I swung—but checked the punch—just in the nick of time. Fortunately, I just grazed her jaw. She fell back, horrified. "Mr. DeCamp!" she screamed. "What in the world is the matter? I'm only going to take your blood pressure!"

"Please forgive me!" I apologized profusely. "I'm really not an ogre—just a coward with instant reflexes. Honest! Guess I'm just jittery about the morning. I'm really sorry!"

She accepted my apology, but no one—I mean no one—in that hospital ever awakened me again, unless they were well out of swinging range.

Sleep was impossible after that, and soon the countdown started toward the exploratory, which had been scheduled for 7 A.M., when the preoperative procedures began.

Wonderful Mickey! He bolstered my morale and it needed bolstering, too! I was really nervous.

I was wheeled to the "holding" place, received a shot, and then was wheeled to the operating room. The shot, meant to relax me, had no effect whatsoever.

In the operating room, my doctor, looking every inch the surgeon in his green cap and gown, smiled down at me and said, "Harry, relax. We're going to take good care of you. Let *me* do all the worrying, okay?"

Then a nurse was strapping my arms to my sides. "This is to prevent you from trying to help us operate," she joked. Both of us burst out laughing.

I started the usual backward countdown: "Ten . . . 9 . . . 8 . . . 7. . . . Then I was gone! This time there was no black void, no light, no fear—just blessed oblivion.

It seemed I was in the recovery room a long, long time. Bess was outside the door buttonholing each person going in or out, begging for any scrap of information. "How is Harry DeCamp doing? My husband . . . ?"

Everyone would just smile at her and reply, "Just fine—he'll be out soon." Poor Bess was a nervous wreck.

Through a haze of pain, my fingers weakly explored my side. *There was no bag!*

Sick as I was, a wave of relief washed over me. I smiled

slyly to myself and thought: *Hey, how about that . . . I still have a bladder! Things must be very good inside.*

My stomach and chest really hurt. My groping fingers touched metal. . . . They had opened me up from the breastbone to the pelvic bone and had hemstitched the vertical cut with wires horizontally (like a double-breasted suit) down my chest to my lower stomach. But . . . *no bag!*

Meanwhile, my doctor had summoned Bess and my sister Hannah to his office. Bess later told me they were scared stiff.

He invited them to sit down "and make yourselves comfortable." From across his desk, looking directly at Bess, he began in his charming accented English, "Mrs. DeCamp, I have bad news. As you know, I was going to take Harry's bladder out if necessary, and a little of the surrounding tissue. I thought that if I had to do that, everything would be fine. But . . ." and here he paused, clasping his hands in front of him on the desk, like a schoolboy, sitting at attention. "When I opened him, I found that the malignancy had spread too extensively behind the bladder. It's invaded all the surrounding tissue. It doesn't look good.

"We have an option, though. . . ."

"What is that, doctor?" Bess asked weakly.

"Mrs. DeCamp, I'd like to send Harry up to Sloan-Kettering in Manhattan. It's the best in the world. We're going to have Dr. ________ (and he named the doctor) look at Harry. He's an excellent man with bladder cancer. You know, he's the surgeon who operated on ________ (a famous American). Harry couldn't be in better hands."

Bess and Hannah looked at each other stunned, as the doctor plunged on. "I feel in sending Harry up there, that maybe there's something he can do with Harry's bladder that I can't do. I hope you'll agree it's worth the try."

"Of course, doctor . . . you know best," Bess replied.

When they left his office, Bess told me much later, she had a sick, empty feeling in her stomach. "Do you suppose he's trying to soften the blow?" she asked.

"What do you mean?" Hannah replied, in a scared voice.

"I mean, maybe he already *knows* that this other doctor won't be able to do any more for Harry than he's done. But he's going through the motions for our benefit!"

"Oh, do you think so, Bess!" Hannah cried, horrified. "Poor Harry!" Then they threw their arms around each other and cried.

Late that afternoon, the doctor came to my room and sat on the foot of my bed. "Harry, don't cross your ankles!" he scolded gently. "It's bad for the circulation." Leaning over, he uncrossed them with one rapid motion. Then he assumed a serious look. "Harry . . ." he faltered, "Harry . . . as you know, we did not remove your bladder. I'm only an expert with a knife—not a *master.* And your condition needs the hands of a master surgeon. I'm arranging for you to go to Memorial Sloan-Kettering Cancer Center in New York. There, Dr. ________ will operate on you (and he named the surgeon he had mentioned to Bess). He's a master with a scalpel. He operated on the famous American. (He actually gave me two famous names.) If anybody can help you, he can, believe me!"

I was excited over the fact that this "great surgeon" would be operating on an ordinary Joe like Harry DeCamp! I thought my doctor was the greatest doctor in the world, and I believed what he was telling me. I was more trusting than Bess. If my doctor said the surgeon could help me, then it was so. He would take care of my problem.

Besides, incredible as it may seem after all this, it still hadn't registered with me that there was any really *serious* trouble inside my body. Whatever was wrong, there was always another step to be taken, another option, and, now, another doctor. Such was my ability to deceive myself, to hear the most dire news in plain English and to somehow not grasp it; or, grasping it, to twist it in a way that would not threaten the idea I had clung to from the start: *Modern medicine would cure me; the doctors with their skill and knowledge would make me like new again.*

"We'll keep you here for the remainder of February, Harry," the doctor was saying. "We'll send you home March first . . . and you'll be in Sloan-Kettering on March fourth."

The balance of February was joke and fun time for me. I was having such a good time, I failed to recognize the subtle change in Mickey's attitude and that of the nurses toward me. It was not until the last day, actually, when I was saying good-bye, that I noticed anything. The rough, tough, street-wise Mickey hugged me and wept softly. I was startled and perplexed.

The nurses all came in to see me off, too. There was lots of hugging and kissing and tears, as I left in a wheelchair, with Bess walking beside me. Why all the fuss? *Why the tears?* It was then, for the first time since I learned I had cancer, that I became just a little apprehensive. . . .

Although it was the beginning of March, the snow was so heavy on the roads that the local ambulance couldn't transport me to New York City, some fifty miles away. It seems there's a law in New York that requires vehicles to have snow tires. Our ambulance driver wouldn't run the risk of a fine, as he had no snow tires. Other means of transportation would have to be found.

My son-in-law Rick volunteered to drive me to Manhattan in his station wagon—snow or no snow. "You've got to get there, don't you?" he asked, sounding determined. "We can prop you up with blankets and pillows in the back seat. I can get through the snow . . . if you can stand it. What do you say?"

"It's okay with me," I replied. Though I didn't say it, I was grateful to my son-in-law for being there when I needed him, for insisting that I allow him to put himself out!

Bess was apprehensive about the trip. She worried about the effect of the bumping on my partially healed chest and stomach. "Hon, there won't be any bumping, there's too much snow on the road," I fibbed.

"What if you guys get stuck in that snow?" she shrilled.

"Mom . . . Rick has good tires," Judy explained patiently. "Don't worry about it, please."

Finally, they got me propped up in the back seat under a ton of pillows and blankets. I think Bess would have thrown a few more on if Rick and Judy hadn't stopped her. Standing in the drive were Judy, and my granddaughters Holly and Heidi, as we took off slowly through the snow.

"Bye, Pop Pop! We love you!" Holly and Heidi yelled. They were still smiling and waving, as the station wagon turned the corner. Suddenly I had a lump in my throat. When would I see them again?

It was a nerve-wracking trip—and painful. Every jolt of the wagon hurt my chest, but I just gritted my teeth and said nothing. No sense upsetting Rick and Bess with something they could do nothing about. I just wanted to get there in one piece. It was tough on Rick, too. That slippery, snowy ride tested all his driving skill—and my confidence in his expertise behind the wheel.

Curiously, I was only slightly apprehensive about what awaited me at Sloan-Kettering. My gosh, if the "great surgeon" had operated on such famous people, he could fix me up for sure!

About two hours later, we finally pulled up outside the massive Sloan-Kettering Center on York Avenue on Manhattan's Upper East Side. We had made it, with no damage to the car or me.

5

The Temple of Medicine

"They . . . worshiped and served the creature rather than the Creator. . . ."

Romans 1:25 RSV

Memorial Sloan-Kettering. The very name is intimidating to the layman. It conjures up visions of a vast temple of science and medicine, sitting in isolated, almost unapproachable grandeur amid rolling lawns.

The reality is a little less than grand. The temple is squeezed into a not-too-wide street on Manhattan's Upper East Side. You don't spy it from afar; you're almost on it when the car turns the corner. There is no opportunity to be properly awed.

Inside, I was seated before a blasé clerk who was going through the usual routine required by hospitals—endless questions for seemingly endless forms. At the risk of sounding cynical, I think they could save everyone time by getting to the point. It all filters down to: "How are you going to pay?" If you can pay, you're in; if you can't, you're out. It's as simple as that.

As you may have gathered by now, I was not impressed by Memorial Sloan-Kettering Cancer Center, despite its formidable reputation (perhaps *because* of the reputation). It was big, all right, but it had the atmosphere of an urban clinic. I had expected it to be sedate and hushed, with a few nurses moving about as quietly as nuns across polished floors, tending old men who all looked like stockbrokers.

Instead, there seemed to be hordes of people of all types milling about: patients, visitors, clerks, nurses. Noise and bustle. *All these people can't have cancer!* I thought as I viewed the crowded admitting area.

The clerk looked up. "All right, Mr. DeCamp. You may go to the eighth floor, the nurses' station. They'll show you to your room." I had passed the important first test: I could pay.

The nurses' station was a large, oblong enclosure in the middle of the eighth floor. As I waited at the desk, a number of patients in bathrobes and hospital gowns went shuffling by, many of them painted zombies. I was to learn that the area surrounding the station was dubbed "the race track"; there the patients stretched their legs or otherwise got themselves going again after surgery.

My room was semiprivate, and very dim. The two beds were placed opposite each other against the inside wall. There was a very small, dark bathroom and a shower stall. A peculiar feature of the room was drawers, built into the wall facing the hallway, for dressings and ointments. These drawers could be opened from both inside the room and outside, in the hall. I never learned the reason for this arrangement, although it may have been for quick access.

In spite of two large, double-hung windows that faced the street, the pale March light was partly blocked by the tall buildings directly across the street.

Looking down from these windows I could see part of the avenue below, filled with banks of dirty snow. Off to the left, a few blocks away, slices of the East River could be seen through the narrow slits between the buildings. Huge boats were gliding up and down the river. I wondered what strange and exotic ports they were bound for, or had visited. The thought filled me with depression. Having been born and raised on the shores of New Jersey, I was used to looking out over the free expanse of the Atlantic, stretching to the horizon—to Europe and Africa, three thousand miles distant.

Now, standing at that window in a hospital on Manhattan's densely packed margins of steel, asphalt, and concrete, I felt as though I were in a huge cage, dropped into a deep chasm. It made me uneasy; I felt like an animal in a zoo.

I had commuted to Manhattan for a year in the 1930s and I often drove through it, so I had no fear of the "big city." But I never liked it. There are too many people and the buildings are too close and too high. To a person like myself, it never seemed quite natural. I needed the beach, the ocean, the wind . . . open spaces.

After a while my roommate came in. I introduced myself, but he barely replied. He got into bed, turned his TV on and lay watching it, as if I weren't there.

"Boy, this cancer bit is a pain in the neck!" I said aloud, to break the ice. "All the tests and treatments! I wonder what the CAT scan will be like. You had it yet?"

No answer. I thought maybe he was shy, so I said, "I've got it in my bladder. What kind of cancer do you have?" I don't think I was being insensitive; after all, we were all there for the same thing. But suddenly he turned to me and snapped: "I don't want to talk about it!" His eyes were fired with hostility. Then he turned back to the television set.

I was shocked and hurt. I had thought that like me, he would derive comfort in talking it out. How terrible it must be to have to keep it all bottled up inside, never mentioning it. You had to feel sorry for a guy like that.

When Bess visited she tried to engage my roommate and his wife in friendly conversation, but she met with the same cold, almost fearful, response. The wife was as taciturn as her husband. It got so bad that whenever I'd try to talk to him about anything, he would turn his face to the wall. Finally I stopped trying. I began to go up to the solarium to look for a few friendly faces.

The second day or so, a tall, slender man of about seventy

stuck his head in the door. "Hi!" he said, with a smile. "How ya doing?"

"Just fine," I replied a bit bowled over by his cheerfulness.

"I'm Kal Eisenbud," he said, coming closer and shaking my hand. "And you?"

"Harry . . . Harry DeCamp." I was warming up to him.

"Nice to meet you, Harry," he said. "Mind if I sit?"

"No . . . no, go right ahead," I replied moving my legs over so he could perch on the edge of my bed.

"Uh . . . I'm in for bladder cancer," I offered. "They'll operate in a few days. . . ."

"Well, Harry," Kal said, "if there's *anything* I can do for you, just holler. Tell the nurse and she'll get me. Okay?"

Seeing my perplexed look, he quickly added, "Oh . . . I'm a volunteer here at the hospital. You know, we've got a great library here. Maybe you'd like to see it now?"

"Sure," I replied, swinging out of bed. Anything to get away from my morose roommate.

Kal, a retired realtor, turned out to be the best thing about Memorial Sloan-Kettering. He stuck out in that drab place like a diamond. Kal was Jewish, and I'm sure he believed in God. But he never talked about religion or preached to anyone or acted as if he were conscious of his goodness. He spent his days visiting patients, comforting them, running errands, and doing favors. His sympathy and interest were genuine. There wasn't a phony bone in Kal Eisenbud's body. I once asked him why he did volunteer work. "To help my fellow man," he replied. Somehow, the way Kal said it, it didn't sound like a United Way poster.

Kal was an optimist; he said he wanted winners, not losers. By that he meant he wanted the patients at Sloan-Kettering to believe they could beat cancer, not give in to it. And with his ready smile and warm handshake and genuine interest, he made you believe you *could* beat it.

I've often wondered just how many patients who passed through that great hospital owe a debt of gratitude to this humble volunteer. I know my stay at Sloan-Kettering was made more bearable because of the support and encouragement of this gentle, caring man.

One day I was in the solarium with Jim, a patient just down the hall from me. We had quickly become friends, though he was a good twenty years my junior. He had bladder cancer too—the whole eighth floor, I understand, had it. Jim was a bright young guy, and we seemed to have a lot in common. He had been an amateur boxer, too, and enjoyed hearing me recount my exploits as Lefty Del Campo, back in the old days. And he also was in the insurance business, as I was.

Anyway, this particular day, we were looking out the window at the Tram, spinning its way on a spider-web cable across the East River at Fifty-Ninth Street, over to Roosevelt Island.

"I was on a tram in Europe," I remarked.

"So was I," Jim said. "I was there for the skiing. When I get out of here I'll go skiing again," he added with grim determination.

"Sure," I replied. There was silence for a minute. I turned and picked up a pamphlet from the coffee table and idly thumbed through it.

"You believe this stuff?" I asked him.

"What's that?" he replied, turning from the window.

"Oh, some religious group left this faith healing literature here. You know, mind over matter. . . ."

"I haven't thought much about it," Jim said. "Did you ever hear of that Israeli guy, Uri something-or-other . . . Uri Geller, I think. He's supposed to be able to bend spoons and things just by thinking about it. Kind of weird."

"I think I saw him on TV once," I replied. "It's hard to believe, but they say it's true. You know, my wife had an aunt who was into Christian Science. She recovered after the doctors told her she was going to die. Even went back to work."

"Well, Har, doctors make mistakes you know. But they usually bury them," he said with a wry smile.

"No . . . Aunt Louise was really in a bad way. I know that for a fact. It was amazing . . . really!" Jim shrugged.

"You're an educated guy, Jim," I said, "do you think that maybe some day we'll be able to control things like cancer with the power of the mind?"

"Maybe, who knows? Say . . . here comes the Tram back again!"

"Wouldn't it be great if you could make yourself well just by using will power, or mind power—whatever," I said. But I had lost Jim. Clearly he was not as interested in the subject as I was.

"It's possible," a voice said behind me. I turned to see Kal Eisenbud standing there. "Mind if I join you guys?"

"Sure thing," I replied, scooting over.

"I think the whole subject of nonmedical healing is fascinating," Kal said. "I've heard of remarkable things happening to people—cancer patients—when they think positively and try to be upbeat." Then seeing Jim's skeptical look, he held up his hands in mock protest and said, "I kid you not, kid!

"Harry," Kal said, turning to me, "I don't care what this guy here thinks, *you* keep thinking positively. I *know* it will do you good! It has to help, believe me. . . ."

"I guess I can use all the help I can get!" I said, thinking of my operation at the end of the week.

"O" Day was fast approaching. Having talked to Bess and the young man whom the doctor had sent, I had pretty much reconciled myself to losing my bladder. Jim, on the other hand, was bitter about the prospect. They had told him they would definitely take his. "It's not fair!" he would fume. "I'm only forty-four! Hell, it's going to knock me out! There's no more sex life after they take it, you know, Har, and I'm too young for that! I've got a young wife. How can I expect her to stick by me? There's not a thing I can do about it, but I sure as hell don't *like* it!"

"Ah . . . come on, Jimmy!" I'd say. "Look, you've been married a long time. Your wife is a very nice person. She's not going to leave you, I *know* that. You're talking nonsense!"

"Maybe . . ." he'd reply.

In a few days, my roommate packed his stuff and left. They had given him some kind of pills and released him. He didn't bother to say good-bye.

He was replaced by a real fireball, a broker-type from Short Hills, New Jersey. This man was hardly friendlier than the first one. He was always on the phone, talking business, cooking up mysterious deals of some kind. He let me know by his officious manner that he was simply too busy to engage in idle chatter. Perhaps I'm wrong, but I got the idea he thought I was his social inferior. At any rate, he kept his distance, and I kept mine.

I never saw the man's wife, and he never had any visitors. He didn't act as though he even had cancer, or else he simply couldn't be bothered by such an inconsequential thing.

It's funny, in an unfunny way, but I've often thought back on that time. I had two roommates at Sloan-Kettering. One was too frightened to even mention the word "cancer"; and the other was too busy making money to acknowledge it. *They're both dead.*

Jim had his operation and evidently made some kind of peace with "the bag." I later heard that, following his release from the hospital, he resumed jogging and even skiing, as he said he would.

Then, I heard through Kal, that Jim's cancer suddenly returned with a vengeance. He was in a hospital in Camden, N.J., near his home, undergoing a new chemotherapy treatment in pill form.

Jim was a fighter all right. But in the end, the cancer killed him just the same.

As I waited for my operation, my one daily visitor—rain, snow or hail—was Bess. Driving the family car the fifty-odd miles from West Long Branch to Manhattan would have been prohibitively expensive—the gas, the bridge and tunnel tolls, plus parking—it was ridiculous. So Bess commuted.

First she would take an hour-and-a-half bus ride up the Garden State Parkway to the Port Authority Bus Terminal on Manhattan's West Side. Then she would fight for a taxi crosstown to Sloan-Kettering. She would stay about two hours, then would race back across town to beat the evening rush-hour traffic back down to the Jersey shore.

She always had a kiss, a warm hug, and a smile for me, but her face was tired and anxious.

"Why do you do it, Hon?" I asked her one day. "You don't have to come up every single day. You look like you need a good rest. Don't come tomorrow. I'll be just fine."

"No, no . . ." she replied, gathering her things together. "I'll come up." Then seeing my disapproving look she grabbed my arm and said, "It's all right, Honey. I'm fine . . . really!"

I wish I could say my doctor's visits were as regular as Bess's. The second or third day, he suddenly appeared and introduced himself. It was the "great surgeon."

"How do you do, Harry?" he said, shaking my hand. "I'm the man who's going to operate on you!"

I was so stunned by the unexpectedness of meeting him, that I was at a loss for words. He wasn't quite what I had expected. He was tall, slender, with graying hair. Rather nice looking, but wearing a nondescript business suit. He impressed me as being capable but slightly officious . . . and busy. He was there not quite five minutes and was suddenly gone—like Elijah taken up by the whirlwind. Although I was to be in the hospital another two-and-a-half weeks I never saw him again. (I have to assume he saw *me* during the operation!)

I can't help comparing my doctor and this surgeon (the Country Mouse and the City Mouse?). My doctor would come in and sit down and explain exactly what was going to happen during your surgery. I felt he was really interested in me, as a person, and what was going to happen to me. And because of his interest he gained my confidence. With the "great surgeon," on the other hand, it was a case of "Hello-and-how-are-you-we're-going-to-take-good-care-of-you-Harry-good-bye."

At the time I put such perfunctory behavior down to his heavy schedule. I mean, he did after all stop by to say hello. But I've never been able to reconcile the fact that Bess—anxious and fearfully concerned about me as she was—never once saw him, or *any* doctor for that matter, during my stay at Sloan-Kettering. What is one to make of that?

I'm just an ordinary Joe, and I don't want to be unfair. But it seems to me that a hospital, no matter how large or crowded or understaffed, should never get to a point where a patient's wife or husband is totally ignored. When that happens I think something is dreadfully wrong somewhere and it ought to be changed. Maybe the Hippocratic oath doesn't extend to relatives.

The nurses (bless them) were a terrific bunch—caring, attentive, and full of jolly humor. It is the memory of their untiring attention, their *humanity,* that redeems for me my stay at Sloan-Kettering. And of course, there was Kal Eisenbud. It's ironic. Kal was the only one who wasn't paid to care about you in the whole darned place, and he cared most of all. Makes you think. . . .

As "O" Day drew near, the tests started: X ray, blood, biopsies, and so on. The CAT scan was the most fascinating, and by this time I was so jaded by tests that it would take something unusual to excite me. I was placed flat on my back on a table and was slowly "fed" into a cylinder, feet first. It resembled a submarine torpedo tube, and worked like some kind of electronic meat slicer. As my body slowly moved into the tube, it was "sliced" with X-ray pictures that gave the doctors detailed cross-section views of various parts of the body that they could read—like the annual rings on tree stumps, only more complicated.

With the massive battery of tests, culminating in the virtually omniscient CAT scan, there was no question of error, no chance for improper diagnosis. I was impressed.

I have somewhat facetiously described Memorial Sloan-Kettering as a temple of medicine and science. But if a temple is where we worship that which we really believe in and depend on, then I think, in that sense, it is true. The physical sciences, including medicine, are what modern society believes in and trusts. Thus, hospitals become "temples" and the doctors, "priests" of a religion that exalts what can be seen, weighed, measured, cured, or otherwise improved upon.

Like most people, I was, without being aware of it, a follower of this modern religion of science and medicine. I placed unquestioning trust in doctors and their almost mystical powers. It was they who held my future, my *life,* in their hands. And when my doctor, in spite of all his skill, said my case was beyond his powers, then I continued on my way, confident as a medieval pilgrim pressing toward a holy shrine, that the next doctor—the "great surgeon"—would surely be the one who would accomplish my healing.

He *had* to work the miracle. My hope had been kept alive because as one option after another failed, there was always another—always *something* that could be done. But now there was only one option left.

I took comfort in the fact that my surgeon had operated on at least one very famous person. Like the rest of us, that person had been a patient on the eighth floor. It's a wonder they didn't declare it a shrine. The stories regarding his most inconsequential comment or action were many and were repeated in awed tones by the nurses. They would point to my nurse, Tippy (not her real name), and would remind me that she had actually attended the famous man. Then they would remind me once again that: "The 'great surgeon,' who is going to operate on you, Mr. DeCamp, also operated on him." Then they'd pause to see if this had had the desired effect. It always did.

In fact, my status in my own mind was swelling by leaps and bounds. *How about that!* I'd think. *I'm traveling the same road as him.*

Finally, it was the day before "O" Day. I was scheduled to go up at 7:30 the next morning. I had psyched myself for the physical change that was to take place. *Harry,* I thought, *this is the last day you'll ever have a bladder.* It was a sobering thought. And depressing.

Then I remembered Bess's words: "Harry, if you have to have it out, you have to have it out." That helped calm the fears that kept popping into my mind as the hours slipped by.

It's curious, but once my fears about losing the bladder were under control, I once more was eaten up by anxiety about the mechanics of its replacement—the bag.

What if it's a sloppy fit and falls off at a political dinner or when I'm walking down a busy street? Suppose it breaks when I'm in a crowded elevator? The picture of these accidents made me break out in a sweat. I wondered: *Will tightening my belt louse it up? Will I smell like a urinal?* And on and on and on.

I was continually asking the nurses about the bag and its mysteries. I asked them right up until bedtime on the eve of "O" Day. "Mr. DeCamp, please don't worry about it!" Tippy said for the umpteenth time. "It will work out, you'll see! You just get a good night's sleep. Tomorrow's the big day!"

Somewhat reassured, I drifted off into a fitful sleep.

It was still dark when they were shaking me awake. "Rise and shine, Mr. DeCamp!" The nurse's voice was maddeningly cheerful as she fussed at my bedside. "We're going to take you down and do a little hemstitching on you!" That was supposed to be funny.

Rubbing my eyes I glanced over at my roommate, the broker. He was lying there with the covers drawn to his chin, shaking. They had injected him with some kind of drug that induced chills and fever that they hoped would kill the cancer cells. It looked to me like it might kill him first.

The nurses left, and I lay there waiting for the orderlies to come and take me. I waited and waited. Nobody came. An hour passed. Then two. The broker was sweating now, and in his near-delirium threw his covers off. A nurse came and covered him up again. He thrashed about on the bed.

Turning to me the nurse said, "They'll be here, Mr. DeCamp. They're probably very busy this morning."

Afternoon came. I got no lunch, since I had been scheduled for surgery. Anticipation had long ago turned to a gnawing anxiety. *Where the devil were they?* Still nobody came.

By mid-afternoon, anxiety had given way to a lethargic depression. I knew they weren't coming for me at all that day.

At about 5 P.M. a doctor fairly exploded into my room. Behind him was a retinue of blank-faced interns. He stood there in a green surgical cap, his face mask dangling around his neck, and blurted out that he was my surgeon's assistant. "Sorry," he panted, "but we had some trouble in the O.R. today. . . . Rest assured, though, Harry (already he was on a first-name basis with me), we'll take you the first thing in the morning. See you tomorrow!"

Away he went, his gear flying behind him, followed by the students in single file. Depressed as I felt, the sight made me chuckle.

True to the assistant's word, in the morning the boys in white came and whisked me to the operating room. The next thing I remember is awakening in the recovery room and being asked: "How do you feel, Mr. DeCamp?"

"Just fine . . ." I lied groggily. With that I found myself being trundled back to my room. I guess traffic was backing up in recovery and they needed the space.

I was still pretty much out of it as they shifted me onto my bed. The sheets felt refreshingly cool on my back and legs, but my chest and stomach hurt badly. I was satisfied to lie there and remain very quiet. How long I lay there before the fear started I'm not sure.

Slowly, like a very small electric current, it started. It began to jiggle up to my brain.

I was thinking about the bag being attached to me. . . .

Now my brain was growing clearer by the second, alerted by that current of fear. My body didn't *feel* any different. The stitches and wires were there all right, *but there was no new sensation.*

A nurse moved into my field of vision. She was pretty: young, tall, slender, and blonde.

"Is there anything we can do to help you, Mr. DeCamp?"

"Nurse. . . . I'm afraid to look. . . . I feel just the same," I whispered hoarsely. "I . . . I want to feel the bag, but . . . I'm afraid. . . ."

Very gently and very softly she said, "Shall we look together?" Suddenly we both laughed (I, feebly) at the humor of the situation. "Thank you . . . but I'd rather do it myself," I smiled. I even managed a sly wink.

"All right, Mr. DeCamp. I'll leave you alone now, but I'll be back in a few minutes." She smiled a strained smile and moved slowly out of range.

I was alone and scared, really scared. I turned my head. My roommate lay under his covers, shaking uncontrollably. There would be no comfort, no support from him. He was having his own problems.

I read a poem once that ends with the line: ". . . one by one, we must all file on, through the narrow aisles of pain." Lying there alone in mortal terror, I knew how true that was!

I stalled for another minute, until I could stand the suspense no longer. Gradually, very gradually, I slipped my hands down. . . .

First my curiously heavy fingers encountered the stitched incision that ran vertically down from my breastbone to the pelvis . . . so sore and tender. My fingers slowly moved across my chest . . . wires. Only this time they were thicker and heavier. *Bigger hospital, bigger wires. . . .* Bumping across the heavy metal that pinched my cut flesh together, my hands moved sharply to the right.

NOTHING. There was no bag!

Oh, dear God, they didn't take it . . . ! Pure joy, like a clear bubbling spring began to well up within me . . . then, just as suddenly, it died.

I'm in big trouble! With the thought came a dreadful sinking sensation like an elevator whose cable had just snapped. *They have left my bladder not because I am better, but because it was too serious . . . too far gone!*

Without warning, tears were streaming down my face, running into my ears and onto the pillow. I was crying and I couldn't stop, crying with my mouth open, like a child cries who has lost control. *I couldn't stop crying!* The racking sobs sent fearful pains through my wounded chest and stomach, and still I couldn't stop.

The young nurse was looking down into my face. I was embarrassed to have her see me crying like a baby, and turned my head away. "They . . . they didn't take it," I sobbed.

"Now, Mr. DeCamp, I'm sure there's a good reason for that. You just wait and see if there isn't. Look at the bright side of it. Someone will be along with a perfectly logical explanation, you'll see." She was patting me and fussing over me, as she would her father—or grandfather. I will always remember her for her kindness.

Desperately I tried to regroup my hopes: *Maybe she's right. It wasn't as serious as they thought. . . . I had one of those remissions cancer patients sometimes get. . . . Who are you kidding, Harry? The nurse is just being kind! You've had it . . . you're dead!*

It was a wild roller-coaster ride between hope and despair; up and down I went.

My hopes had been pinned on the "great surgeon." He was going to be my savior. He was going to remove the diseased bladder and with it that terrible cancer. But he hadn't seen fit to take it. I still had my bladder . . . and that cancer. It was growing . . . spreading. The surgeon was my last hope. Now, suddenly, there was no hope. *There was no hope at all!*

That couldn't be true! I would just have to wait, try to be patient and calm, until someone came to explain.

At about 5:30, the assistant arrived. This time his pace was much slower, and he was somber. I noticed that his retinue was missing.

Sitting on the side of my bed he inquired, "How are you feeling, Harry?"

"I'm not so good. I hurt. . . ." I croaked through parched lips. You . . . didn't remove my bladder!" I blurted. "Why?"

There was silence, and then he spoke. "Harry . . . when we opened you up, we found that the cancer had spread so extensively throughout the tissue of your body . . . an operation was impossible. Had we cut away all the cancerous tissue, well . . . we would have literally cut you in half!

"Harry . . . there is no other way to tell you—your cancer is inoperable. I'm very, very sorry, but there was nothing we could do. . . ."

"How . . . much . . . time do I have?"

"Again, Harry, I must be honest," the doctor was saying. "We can promise you *no* time. Not a week . . . not a month . . . not six months. We can't promise you any time."

I had been condemned to die.

They let Bess in to see me. I looked into her face; her eyes searched mine. "How do you feel, Hon? Was the doctor here? What did he say?" I could always read her; she knew it was bad news.

"I'm dead."

"What do you mean, you're dead?"

"He says there's no hope, Bess. I'm inoperable. I'm going to die."

Bess's face was falling apart. The words were destroying her, as the cancer was destroying me. Tears were in her eyes, and she reached down to hug me.

"Oh . . . oh . . . Har!" she sobbed into my shoulder. Now the tears were streaming down my face again, as she clung to me, like a scared little girl.

After a few minutes, I felt her stiffen. Suddenly she sat up, wiping her eyes, with a methodical, almost angry gesture. "Harry," she announced, "there are lots of things we can do! There's chemotherapy. There's all sorts of things!"

She stopped as our eyes locked in an awful moment of realization. We didn't have to say it—we both knew there was no way out. *It was final . . . so very, very final!*

The balance of March was a nightmare, punctuated by "meals" of jello and ginger ale, which I could not get down. My appetite had been decreasing to the point of none. I just couldn't eat. Everything smelled and tasted bad.

I have since learned that many cancer patients die, not from the disease itself, but from the effects of malnutrition. I *tried* to eat, but the sight and smell of food sickened me and made me gag. Finally, I stopped trying.

I don't remember anyone except Bess scolding me about my failure to eat, though my weight dropped steadily. The hospital staff went to great lengths to record my swift decline. A little mobile crane would be wheeled alongside my bed. Two slats would be placed on either side of me. The sheet would be rolled over the slats, and they would then crank me up in the air and weigh me—like a steer.

It was almost as if they regarded my fast as the usual thing. Nothing to get excited about. Oh, there were shots to put me to sleep for six or eight hours at a stretch, but that was about the extent of it.

Periodically, doctors would come in and look at me and then walk out again. It was as if I were a textbook problem to them, one they hadn't been able to solve or explain. At other times, I felt like a frog being studied—just prior to dissection.

I got into a crazy, silly state of mind. I've always been that way. The more grim the situation gets, the more humor I automatically try to wring out of it. I'm convinced that if a mugger had a gun to my head and was going to pull the trigger in the next five seconds, I'd make some wisecrack.

So, during those final, bleak days at Sloan-Kettering, as spiritually crushed as I was, I became cynically humorous with the surgeon's assistant and his retinue of interns. They looked for all the world like the Seven Dwarfs, trooping in behind him. I almost expected them to break into a chorus or two of "Heigh Ho! Heigh Ho," as they made their rounds.

I even named them Smiley, Dopey, Grumpy, Sleepy, Doc, etc., and addressed them as such. It was disrespectful, and I never elicited so much as a smile from one of them, or any response for that matter. (A punch in the nose would have indicated they were at least human.) I redubbed them the Doomsday Boys, but kept *that* to myself.

Of course, my silliness and teasing were all false bravado, a kind of shaky mental seawall to keep me from being engulfed by that monstrous wave, Hopelessness.

I now joined the small army of zombies, shuffling around "the race track." I was a zombie, too. I remember one day, dragging myself around the circle on Judy's arm. I was really feeling sorry for myself. "Judy," I said, "if I fall over . . . catch me."

If I thought she'd respond with sympathy I was wrong. "If you fall over, I'm getting out of the way! You're too darned big to hold up, Dad!"

"What's the use?" I said, pitifully.

Judy stopped dead in her tracks, her eyes blazing. She was oblivious to the other patients and nurses who were staring.

"What's this stuff? First you were telling me, 'I'm not going to quit. I'm going to beat this!' Now you're going to curl up and *die?*"

"This is different!" I protested feebly.

"How is it different?" she asked, hands planted firmly on her hips. She wasn't letting me off the hook.

"The doctors can't do anything for me."

"So what? They told the man in the next bed that, too. And you were yelling at *him,* because he wanted to give up. That was just a few weeks ago, Dad."

I stood there with my head bowed. "Dad . . . you told me never to be a quitter. Whenever I failed a test, or lost a part in a play, you told me to hang in there, didn't you? Now, take your own advice!

"So maybe you've got six weeks. Are you going to spend it sitting in bed, crying? Or are you going to get up and move around and *live* that last six weeks?"

That was hard to take from my own daughter. Judy knew that Bess couldn't say it to me, so she had to.

I'm grateful that she was there for me and was strong enough to set me straight. It's called "tough love."

I developed a prolonged attack of hiccoughs, probably brought on by my failure to eat. I couldn't stop them, nor could the doctors. Finally, a nurse said, "Here. Put this over your mouth and breathe in and out." It was a brown paper bag. It worked. This has always struck me as hilarious, that here I was in a multi-million dollar medical temple, a citadel of healing, with all the latest equipment and the top medical brains in the country. Yet I had to resort to the old brown paper bag routine to cure hiccoughs. I still laugh every time I think of it.

Friends from West Long Branch began to phone me. Former business associates from New York, whom I hadn't seen in years, showed up to visit me. Evidently, word was getting around that old Har wasn't long for this world. The visits were short and uncomfortable. I felt more sorry for the visitors than they did for me.

One day Bess phoned me from downstairs. "Go to the window and look down, Harry!"

I shuffled over to the window and looked down to the street. Eight floors below were Rick and Judy standing on York Avenue with Heidi and Holly. Judy was pointing up toward the window. Suddenly the girls spotted me and broke into big smiles and began to wave. How beautiful they looked! I'd have given anything then to have been able to reach down out of that window and scoop them up into my arms.

Bess explained that they had come to Manhattan ostensibly to visit the Museum of Natural History. The children didn't know it of course, but they were waving good-bye to Pop Pop. Maybe they sensed something was amiss, or why couldn't they come up and talk to Pop Pop and sit on his lap? But they were so very, very young. . . .

Tears sprang into my eyes. *I would never see them grow up . . . never see them marry. I would not see them six months from now.*

Then they all turned and walked away, down the bare March street. I tried to burn the bittersweet sight of the retreating figures into my mind, to store it up like a photograph, for the dark days to come.

As they continued to move away, I leaned as far to the window as I could, straining to hang onto the sight. Suddenly I had an urge to cry out, to stop them! It seemed as though they were walking out of my life, taking joy and health, warmth and laughter with them!

I pictured them going on for years, all of them, enjoying one another, enjoying life. Sadly I wondered if they would think of me. Surely sometimes . . . in those future years they would talk fondly of me? I tried to picture that time in the distant future that would exist without me, but I couldn't. . . .

I was jolted sharply back to reality, when I banged my head on the glass, straining for that last look.

After that day I cried very easily. The tears just seemed to flow, regardless of the reason, or for no reason. It was embarrassing. Later I found out through Jim that everyone on the eighth floor who knew me was whispering: "Harry De-Camp is not going to make it. Did you know that?"

On March 29, they told me I could go home the first of

April. Bess arranged for our hometown ambulance to come to New York and take me back home to West Long Branch. They gave us a supply of sleeping pills and painkillers as big as your thumbnail and wished me luck.

It was going to be a painful journey, but one to which I eagerly looked forward. I had come to Sloan-Kettering so full of hope for my life. Now I was going home to die. With grim humor I realized it would be April Fools' Day. The joke was on me.

6

The Healing

". . . and when he saw Jesus, he fell on his face and besought him, 'Lord, if you will, you can make me clean.' And he stretched out his hand, and touched him, saying, 'I will; be clean.' "

Luke 5:12, 13 RSV

That first night home, Bess decided she would sleep in another room, so as not to disturb me.

The minute I turned off the light and slid down under the covers, my heart began to pound. I felt as though I were *smothering.* Reaching over, I fumbled for the light switch. The cheerful glow of the bedlamp made me feel a little better. After a minute, I snuggled down under the covers again and stared at the ceiling. Then it came again, that awful feeling of not being able to breathe! My chest felt constricted, as if someone were sitting on me; my breath came in gasps. Panic gripped me. *I had to sit up or I'd die!*

I struggled up onto my elbow. My sutures were pulling painfully and my heart was thumping like it would pound through my chest. Sweat popped out on my forehead. Throwing the covers back, I lurched off the bed and stood up, my legs trembling, my brain suddenly giddy. Breathing deeply a few times, I felt the terrible pressure in my chest subsiding.

Slipping into my robe with some difficulty, I plodded into

the living room and turned the light on. I sank into my easy chair with a deep sigh. What was wrong with me? Was it panic? Was it stark fear? That feeling of suffocation was terrible. But now, sitting up, with the light on, I felt much better.

Bess came out of the guest room. "Will you turn the TV on for me?" I asked.

"What's the matter?" she asked, flicking the switch.

"I don't know. I can't seem to lie down. I feel just like I'm smothering."

On the TV screen Paul Henreid lit up two cigarettes and handed one to Bette Davis.

"What do you mean, 'smothering'?"

"Just what I said," I replied. "I can't breathe. I don't know why."

Bess seemed unsure of how to take this. What could she do about this latest crisis? Nothing really. . . .

Now Bette Davis was telling Paul Henreid not to ask for the moon when they had the stars. The camera panned the trees and the starry sky. . . .

"Bess, you go back to bed. I'll be all right."

Bess glanced absently at the TV as the music came up. "You want to sleep in here tonight, Hon?" she asked.

"I'll have to, I think. I just can't lie down."

She went and got me two pillows and some blankets and covered me up. "Try to get some sleep now, Har, okay?"

"Okay . . . but I'll just watch TV for a while first. Oh . . . leave the light on, will you?" Bess turned and looked at me dubiously for a second, then went back to bed.

I spent the night propped in that easy chair, and the next night, and the next . . . and God knows how many other nights and days.

I was still unable to eat, and my weight plummeted. Food smelled terrible; the thought of it made me gag. Bess would bring me some eggs and toast, but I couldn't even look at the stuff. I'd turn my head and wave her away, fighting my revulsion.

"Harry!" she would say, her voice shrilling slightly, as it did when she was anxious, "I don't *care* if you're not hungry! EAT!" But for once her pleading and coaxing were in vain. My inability to sleep or eat was speeding up the otherwise slow, insidious process of deterioration. My decline now was swift and sure.

I sat propped in that easy chair in our living room and stared at meaningless images on the TV screen twenty-four hours a day . . . *dying.*

I felt miserable and sorry for myself. Why did I have to die? *Why me, God?* I demanded. *Why not some real sinners? Why not muggers, rapists, murderers, child molesters? Was I such a bad guy? I always took care of my family. . . . Why?*

But no answer came. The idiotic laughter of contestants on some silly game show or other underscored the pointlessness, the stupidity, of what was happening to me. The laughter seemed to mock me. *That it should end like this. . . .*

So I complained to God. I was angry at Him. Paradoxically, and though I was hardly conscious of it at the time, my anger was my first genuine contact with God.

I had a nodding acquaintance with the Deity. As I've said, I believed He existed. Sometimes I thought of Him "out there"—a cold, remote Being in space who kept the cosmos running. At other times, He would seem a bit closer, but like a shadowy figure moving behind the scenery of life. Either way, God had nothing to do with Harry DeCamp or his problems.

Now I began to wonder if somehow I might make contact with God. How could I do it? I thought about church. But as I've explained, I never cared for church people or the whole idea of church. I didn't intend to change now. Even if I had wanted to go (which I didn't), I would have felt like a hypocrite. I reasoned that even if God helped people in trouble (which I wasn't at all sure of), He certainly wouldn't help *me,* after I had ignored Him all my life. It just didn't seem logical or fair. I have always believed in the law of retribution: you do something, you pay the price. I was now paying the price of having ignored God for sixty-six years. There would be no help forthcoming for the likes of Harry De-Camp.

So I just sat there in that easy chair, stoically staring at TV reruns and old movies. I didn't really see or hear what was on the screen, my mind was always on myself and the insidious cancer, growing and gnawing away at my insides.

I pictured the cancer cells as ugly, squiggly things that resembled varicose veins; they were growing, multiplying, attaching themselves to my bladder, my kidneys, my liver. . . .

At times, a cold sweat would suddenly break out and run down my chest in rivulets, as I realized death was racing toward me at breakneck speed.

A bizarre image kept flashing on and off in my brain, like a nightmarish neon sign: *I was lying in an open casket, my head cradled on white satin. No breath stirred in my nostrils, no flush of life was in my cheek. I was stiff and cold and composed, my hands folded over one another, unmoving as stone, their color the color of clay. . . .*

This image would alternate with scenes from my life. Vividly I would see a tiny Judy sitting on my chest, reaching down to squeeze my cheeks and nose with pudgy baby hands. How dear, how bittersweet that was!

But mostly, the scenes were dark ones in which I would be saying cutting things to Bess or a friend, things I shouldn't have said. There was one that kept recurring over and over:

It was Christmas Eve in the late 1940s and I am stumbling in the door, tipsy from an office party, when I should have been home earlier to help Bess and Judy trim the tree. Bess is watching me tight-lipped, and little Judy has a scared, uncomprehending look in her dark eyes. Why did I do it? Why didn't I come home? It had happened a lifetime ago, and yet I could have cried remembering—wanting to go back and do it all over, do it right. But it was too late . . . too late!

With the rising of the sun, these disturbing visions became less frequent. Is it any wonder I began to dread seeing the night come? The encroaching darkness reminded me of death that was rushing at me, and the night shadows spawned those dark fantasies.

Inevitably, my mind got around to the idea of suicide. These grim thoughts would materialize to haunt me in the hours between midnight and daybreak. I kept a .22 caliber target pistol in the bedroom. It was loaded with ten bullets. One was all that I would need. I pictured myself taking it out of the drawer, holding the cold metal against my temple and pulling the trigger. . . .

What could be simpler, quicker? It would be over in an instant. Then the grisly image would fade, to be replaced by one in which I was taking an overdose of sleeping pills. No, it would be sleeping pills and liquor, an even more deadly combination. I would simply go to sleep, fade away. It would save everyone time, trouble, and headaches.

This image would be bumped out of my brain by one of Judy, standing in the corridor of Sloan-Kettering scolding me: *"Dad, you told me never to be a quitter! Now take your own advice!"*

"Harry," I told myself, "you're going crazy! What do you do now?"

My natural instinct was against being a quitter. I had always been a fighter, a survivor, the guy who wasn't afraid to take a chance, the guy who always managed to bounce back. So I decided if I was going to go down, I'd go down fighting, with dignity—like a man.

Except for a dull ache in the area of my bladder, I wasn't in much pain. (Actually, I have always had a high tolerance for pain of any kind.) So once I made up my mind that I wouldn't take the easy way out of this no-win situation, I decided to go all the way. I refused to take the painkillers or the sleeping pills they had given me at Sloan-Kettering. It was the life instinct in me, fighting to maintain itself. I didn't want my brain fogged up; I didn't want drugs of any kind in my body. I wanted to be fully aware of every precious moment of life I had left.

Visitors would drop in. Their reactions were so typical, so obvious. They would invariably talk in low tones, as if they were in a funeral parlor. And when they spoke to Bess about me, it was usually in the *past tense.* What really irked me was that I was present during these conversations, and they'd talk as though I weren't there.

"Poor, Harry!" they'd say. "He was such a big man! He was so active and highly respected! My, how much weight he's lost! He looks so thin! How are *you* coping, Bess?"

Why they didn't ask me, I'll never know. It never occurred to them to ask Harry how he was feeling, or what he was thinking. Obviously, since I was dying, or, for all practical purposes, was already dead, I guess they thought I had no ideas or feelings.

Once a friend came to visit. He sat there a while, commiserating with me and then said, "Well, Har . . . we've all got to pay for the wrongs we've done! Now it's your turn!"

His tone of voice as he said this fairly oozed self-righteousness—and this from one of the biggest carousers in town. I knew, because I had hung out with him!

"You ____!" I bellowed. "You talk that way to me? You can just get the ____ out of my house!" He beat a hasty retreat. I no longer considered him my friend.

Visits from Rick, Judy and the grandchildren, of course, were always enjoyable. I loved holding Heidi and Holly on my lap, cuddling them, playing games. Judy and Rick would fill us in on their day-to-day activities, the usual family talk. But behind the cheerful conversation was the forbidden, unspoken thought: *Dad's dying of cancer, but we won't talk about it.*

Their visits were precious and painful to me at the same time. But I was determined not to let them know the sadness that lay heavy on my heart. It was the sadness of parting.

Flowers and fruit baskets began arriving from expected people and places—and from unexpected people and places. I was surprised, and touched by the concern they showed. A relative told me that a group of Roman Catholic nuns in a convent in Plainfield, New Jersey, was saying masses for me, and that they would continue for a solid year. I was touched by that too, though I wouldn't be around three months from now, let alone a year. Their prayers, I feared, would be wasted.

It seemed everybody was praying for me, both Protestants and Catholics, church groups and nonchurch groups. They were all bombarding heaven with intercessory prayers for my healing! Being scientific-minded, that struck me as peculiar. They were too late in asking Him for old Har. Because I had ignored Him, God wasn't going to answer their prayers any more than He was going to answer mine. It was all so much well-meant but wasted effort!

Get well cards began coming, and in large numbers. Like the prayers, they were well meant, but pointless. Even the name, "get well card," implies they are for people who are getting well, the fortunate ones who have a future. They aren't intended for the dying.

One of them arrived from a relative, Eleanor, a distant cousin we knew only casually. She had always impressed me as a sincerely religious person, and a good woman. At the bottom of her card she had scrawled the message: "With God all things are possible."

I put her card on the stack with the others, but for some reason the line stuck in my mind like a needle. I kept going back to it, rereading it. "*All* things are possible. . . ." Where had I read it before? I thought it might be from the Bible. (Later I discovered that it is from the Bible—Matthew 19:26.) I found myself repeating the words over and over, and I didn't know why. I was not religious. Why was I so taken by the line? I was soon to find out.

The mail brought a magazine called *Guideposts,* published by Norman Vincent Peale, the famous preacher and author of *The Power of Positive Thinking.* In that little magazine were two stories that were to turn my world upside down—or I might better say, rightside up.

On the cover was the picture of a smiling couple. A blurb said: "Hopeless, the doctors told Milly Gordon. But this well-known writing team refused to accept their diagnosis." "Hopeless. . . ." That first word jarred me. That's what *I* was, too. That's what the doctors had said about *me!*

Intrigued, I opened the magazine and began to read.

Milly Gordon and her husband, Gordon, were a best-selling writing team whose books had sold in the millions. Their book, *That Darn Cat* was turned into a movie by Walt Disney and was a box office smash. Then in 1974, Milly came down with a serious heart condition. Before she could recover from that tragic development, it was discovered that she also had bone cancer. The doctors gave the Gordons the bad news, along with painkillers and sent her home to die. Just like me.

But, according to the story, Milly Gordon "never for a moment accepted the verdict of the doctors." Milly had faith. She believed in miracles and in the accounts of the healings performed by Jesus in the New Testament.

The story quoted her as saying: "Just because Jesus doesn't walk the earth today, doesn't mean that healing in the twentieth century, can't be undertaken in His name."*

That really made me think. Even though I had never had any use for the church, Jesus Christ had always been an appealing figure to me, as He is to nearly everyone, believers and unbelievers alike. Wistfully I thought how wonderful it would be if that statement were only true—if somehow the healing power of Christ were really active in the world today and available to someone like me. But the concept was fantastic, too good to be true.

Besides, as I've indicated, I prided myself on being a rationalist—a true child of the scientific age. I didn't know much about religion, but I did know that modern theology had fallen into step with science and had pretty much dis-

* "You Only Have to Believe," by Charlotte Hutchison, *Guideposts,* March 1978.

pensed with the idea of miracles as outmoded, a relic of the Dark Ages.

So why did I continue to read that story? I'm not sure, but I felt as if someone had thrown me a life preserver. Eagerly, almost desperately, I read on. According to the story, Milly Gordon eventually was healed of her heart problem and her cancer because of prayer and ". . . really massive doses of faith."

The trouble was, I didn't know anything about prayer or faith. I knew the Lord's Prayer, but I had said it only sparingly in the last few years. The very word *prayer* conjured up childhood memories of black-robed ministers sending up unbearably long pleas to God in stilted Elizabethan English, while I fidgeted in a pew. I couldn't picture myself doing *that.*

If only prayers and miracles were possible. . . . But, no, these ideas contradicted everything I believed about science, logic, and the nature of reality. Everything in the universe operates according to strict, natural law, which never changes or deviates one iota. If God were to cause a miracle of healing, wouldn't that mean He would be contradicting or violating His own laws of nature?

But, I reasoned, maybe it had something to do with a higher law—something we didn't yet know about, something like mind-over-matter. The idea triggered a memory of my conversation with Jim that day at Sloan-Kettering. I recalled his disinterest in the ideas of the power of the mind and positive thinking. But then Kal Eisenbud had told me that thinking positively could help me. Hadn't he said he had heard of cases where people were actually cured by thinking good positive thoughts? I thought of Bess's Aunt Louise getting out of her deathbed and going back to work. Just like Milly Gordon in the *Guideposts* story. . . .

In the same issue of *Guideposts* was an article, "In Tune With the Infinite," by Lew Miller.* A picture of the author

* Adapted from *Your Divine Connection* by Lew Miller; Celestial Arts, 1977.

graced the title page. He seemed to be about my age. The article explained that Lew Miller was a World War II veteran who had been seriously wounded and reduced to a near-vegetable existence, barely able to move, see, talk, or hear. I looked at Miller's picture again. He seemed a perfectly normal, middle-aged man with a rather kind, almost placid look about him.

In the story Miller told how he had tried to get his wasted, pain-racked body moving. He would struggle out of bed—all ninety pounds of him—and would fall flat on his face. Yet, according to his account, through faith, Lew Miller was also healed!

His healing was accomplished when Miller stumbled onto a revolutionary idea. During one of his rare periods of mental relaxation, he began to relive the athletic triumphs of his school days. *"In every instance,"* Miller recalled, *"I had pictured that success beforehand.* The more vivid the picture and the greater the faith I had in it, the greater the degree of success."

That sounded like good old Kal Eisenbud telling me to think positively. But Miller quoted Jesus: "Whatever you ask in prayer, believe that you receive it, and you will" (Mark 11:24, RSV). When I read that I put the magazine down. I never knew that Jesus Christ had said something like that! It was a mind-blowing idea! (Evidently Miller thought it was mind-blowing too, because he quoted the profound sentence *twice* in that story!)

There's a way out! I thought, *a way to beat this cancer!*

Excitedly I called to Bess. "Honey, have you read these stories in *Guideposts?*" Then before she could answer, I blurted out, "If God can do these things for these people, I'll bet He can heal me, too!"

"I'm sure he can, Har," replied Bess in a way that told me she didn't really believe it. In the next day or so, Bess encouraged me as I read and reread those two stories. Not that it was going to make any real difference, but it might keep my spirits up. I could tell what she really thought by her telephone conversations to her friends.

I couldn't blame her. She'd been through so much. And her mother had been a nurse. Doctors and medicine and the grim details of various diseases—and death—had been the norm in Bess's upbringing. It was evident to me that Bess was humoring me, but definitely not believing. Cancer to her, as it is to most people, is synonymous with death. You contract cancer, you die! It was that simple!

But I would not lay that little magazine down. It was like a lifeline, tossed to a drowning man. I was that drowning man! I read and reread those stories, and then read them again, over and over and over.... Their words were branded on my brain. It was so uplifting to me, just to think of having some chance, *any* chance! It was enthralling!

I started to pray. I did not know how, but I prayed anyway! I worked at it, hour after hour, day after day. But nothing happened. It seemed as if my words just bounced off the ceiling. Milly Gordon had talked about knocking on God's door with prayer, and I was doing that. Yet, was I *really* expecting Him to answer? No . . . I was only kidding myself. I had been a scoffer, a skeptic for too many years.

If these people did it, I thought, *and it worked for them, then there has to be something that they did that I'm missing. What?*

Both Milly Gordon and Lew Miller talked about faith and prayer and believing. But how do you get to the point where you believe or have faith? How was I supposed to pray? I was back to square one....

I reread the Miller story. In his article Miller said that picturing the desired result of something, or imaging, isn't a new technique. Even Jim Thorpe the famous athlete practiced it, as had a number of other famous people. Miller suggested to the reader the device of picturing a movie screen in your head, with the thing you desire being shown as a little movie.

But what would a mini-moving picture in my mind have

to do with God? How could I tap into God's power with that? Somehow I couldn't make the connection.

Then, during one of my midnight-to-sunrise sessions in front of the TV set, watching old movies, a thought popped into my mind—just like a piece of bread pops up in a toaster. The analogy or imaging device that would work for me, wasn't a movie screen—*it was a TV transmission!*

Those TV programs had to originate at a base station, a power source, didn't they? They then were sent out into the ether. How do we receive them? We first must have a TV set, a receiver. Then we must turn the set *on.* Then we must *tune* to a *particular* channel. When we did all this, we would then receive a program, as would 30 million other people if they chose the same program.

Isn't that the way with God's power? I asked myself excitedly. *God's power goes out into the ether from a "base station." It too is there for the taking, isn't it? If we just "tune in."*

My big problem was: how do I get it? How do I "tune in"? Through faith. That was what I was lacking: FAITH.

First, I imagined a little TV screen in my head. Then I began to visualize God, not as some ethereal Being way up there in the wild blue yonder, but right there, alongside me. I mean literally. When I "prayed" I didn't look *up;* I looked at the chair *beside* me, and talked to God like a friend. (Why not? I was beginning to realize He was the best Friend I could ever have!) I was carrying on a nonstop, marathon conversation with God! It was wonderful! Exciting! It was glorious!

I was only following Milly Gordon's advice. She had said, "Most of the time we knock on the door so timidly and open it just a little crack." So I began to knock on God's door *boldly!* "Dear God, please heal me of my cancer!" I prayed. "I thank You for my healing! And, Lord, I also thank You for my life. I thank You for my eyesight, I thank You for my hearing, I thank You for my family. . . ." There were no fancy words or pious phrases; it was just simple talk from a plain Joe.

So I had finally asked God, the Ruler of the universe, the Creator of the world and all that is in it (including Harry DeCamp) to heal me of cancer. I reasoned that if Milly Gordon and Lew Miller had been healed by asking in faith, then so could I. What's more, I *thanked* Him for my healing, even though nothing was happening.

You might think that strange. But, you see, as I later found out through reading my Bible, believing when you can't see any change in the situation is what faith is all about. Otherwise, if you could see the result right off the bat, there wouldn't be any trick to it at all! As Paul said so aptly: "Faith is the substance of things hoped for, the evidence of things not seen" (Hebrews 11:1). Now I had a measure of faith, activated by the technique of mentally imaging God on that little TV screen in my head. And I believed. Oh, how I believed! And what a blessed thing it was to believe. It was like a path out of the wilderness! And it was all so simple, so obvious! Why hadn't it occurred to me before?

On that little mental TV screen, I pictured myself getting out of that chair and walking, riding my bicycle, driving my car, playing golf!

More importantly, I began to visualize the white blood cells—they seemed like little round squiggly things—cascading down from my shoulders and going through all the tissues and organs of my body, attacking the cancer cells. Down my legs they would move, then back up through the tissues and organs once again, to my head. Then they would sweep down again, resting at my shoulders, awaiting the next charge.

Curiously, a tiny little Jesus, no bigger than a minute, was leading the charge of the heroic white blood cells, was walking with vigor and purpose through my body with a staff in His hand. Where had He come from, this little Jesus? I hadn't asked God to send Him. I hadn't intended to "image" Him. But suddenly He had been there. And I accepted Him without question. What a wonderful feeling of security and strength that image of a little Christ within me gave!

As those white blood cells, led by Christ, raced around, they traveled as an army. They would seek out the enemy—the ugly, vein-like cancer cells—and pounce on them, totally destroying them. I could actually see this happening.

I ran this "picture" through my mind hundreds of times every day and night. I talked with God all day and night. I began to feel that I, not the cancer, was now in control. That in itself was a tremendous morale booster.

One day, about two weeks after I had begun my prayer and imaging program, I was talking to God one afternoon about four o'clock. "Lord," I said, "I know I must have some kind of future. And You're going to work it out for me, in some way, in some shape or form. You know what I want You to do for me. You know my heart and my feelings, Lord. You're the only One who can help me now. It's all in Your hands. . . ."

All at once, something wonderful happened that had never happened before in all of my prayer conversations. A strange, peaceful feeling came over me—*invaded* me.

First fear went—like water draining out of a tub; then, tension went. (My body had been full of tension; everybody had been telling me for weeks that I was going to die and I believed them. My mind and body were just full of tension and fear, like a coiled spring.)

I had been praying and praying, knocking on God's door for days—weeks—and suddenly the door had swung open. Don't ask me how I knew it, but in that wonderful, magical moment I *knew;* I *felt* in the very core of my being that I had been *healed.*

How can I describe that feeling of utter relief? It was as if I had been strapped in the electric chair, waiting for the executioner to pull the switch. But God had stepped in and said, "No!" And He had unstrapped me and told me I was free to go.

I remember once, as a child of nine, I nearly drowned

while on a Sunday school picnic. I had dived into a lake that was deeper than I had expected. I vividly recall seeing a boat in the distance. I was yelling and thrashing, but I couldn't get their attention, and I couldn't seem to move toward them. And I knew I was going to die.

Then suddenly, my foot brushed against something under the water—an upright pipe. I put my big toe in the open tip of that pipe. That tiny opening gave me just the support (the toehold, if you'll pardon the pun) that I needed to push myself up and keep afloat until the boat reached me. When I put my toe in that pipe, I knew instantly that I wasn't going to die after all. *That's* what it was like that May afternoon in 1978.

I began to get hungry. That in itself was evidence that something had happened—I had eaten next to nothing for almost six weeks.

"Bess! Bess!" I called. "Come, quick!" Bess came hurrying into the living room.

"What's the matter?" she asked, looking all breathless and scared. (I hadn't meant to frighten her.)

"I'm hungry!" In fact, by that time I was ravenous!

"How about some nice hot tea and crackers?" Bess asked. This would have been a banquet for me, and Bess knew it.

"No, ma'm, I want something solid," I shot back, hardly able to contain my glee.

"Oh? I suppose you want me to run out and get a submarine sandwich?" Bess asked with a trace of sarcasm. She was in no mood for games. (Bess had been under a severe strain for weeks, and it was showing.)

"Yes, I would," I replied.

Out went Bess, and in a short time she returned with a huge submarine sandwich—one of those miniature loaves of Italian bread, split lengthwise down the middle and filled with Italian cheese, meat, lettuce, sliced tomatoes and sprinkled with vinegar and oil. It was a large meal in itself, and I ate the whole thing—with relish!

Bess was not only astounded, she was flabbergasted! She

had been trying for weeks to get me to eat something, anything. And now, at last I had devoured a whole sub in a few minutes! Later that same evening, I surprised Bess again when I ate a snack and drank some milk. (This had been my normal routine before I came down with cancer; always a snack and milk before bed.)

That food tasted delicious; there was never a thought about not being able to keep it down. I was eating like a healthy person.

About midnight I decided to go to bed. "I'll bring your pillows and blankets, Har," Bess said.

"No, don't bother," I replied. "I'm going to sleep in bed for a change. I've had enough of that easy chair!"

Bess looked at me strangely. I couldn't blame her. I had been propped in that easy chair every night since I came home; now I blithely announced I was going to bed like any normal person!

She helped me into the bedroom, and in a few minutes (for the first time in weeks) I slid between the clean sheets, stretching myself full length. It felt *so good!* I lay there a few minutes, savoring the experience. Here I was lying on my back, breathing in a perfectly normal fashion. There was no hint of tension, no struggle to breathe. Instead, I was aware of my chest rising and falling in relaxed, rhythmic fashion. I thanked God that I could do something as simple as lying on my back in bed, breathing normally—things that most people take for granted. It was a further sign that He had indeed healed me.

Totally relaxed, with all fear and tension and pain gone from mind and body, and thanking the Lord, I fell into a very sound sleep.

The following morning I was able to eat a good breakfast. Then Bess helped me to take a walk, inside the house. It was wonderful to be on my feet, moving again, wonderful to know the free feeling of being healed.

I continued talking with God, mostly to myself, in the "closet" of my heart and mind, but very seriously. I talked to Him, on and on and on. I now wonder, thinking back on it, why He didn't turn me off, just to get a rest. I was on a real talking binge. Can you blame me? I had been reprieved. I was back from the dead!

I promised God that because He had been kind enough to heal me—a nonreligious individual—I would shout His praises from the housetops. Now, when you make a promise to God, you had better be prepared to fulfill it; He does not forget. He holds you to it, and He doesn't fool around. But more of this later. . . .

About three days after my healing, I was sitting in my easy chair, thanking God and imaging my body as all healed. Then, quite unexpectedly again, I imaged Christ on that mental TV screen. He was standing across the room, next to the television set. I could see His eyes, piercing yet soft. I could not tell you their color, because I saw all this in my mind's eye. He was wearing a white robe and was walking toward me. He seemed to walk right into me; and again I felt that wonderful feeling of wholeness and utter peace. In that moment I experienced the truth of Christ's words (words that I was to read only later): "In that day you will know that I am in my Father, and you in me, and I in you" (John 14:20, RSV).

The Lord has many ways of reaching us. I had no one to tell me I was a sinner. But I had felt my utter need of God; I had been let down—abandoned, if you will—by everything I had trusted in life: my health, my strength, my intellect, my dependence on doctors. Nothing and no one—not even my beloved Bess and my family—could help me. I had been cut off from every source of help and hope. And then, when my back was pinned against the proverbial wall, when I was jammed against that wall so tight that I couldn't even move my head a fraction of an inch, I had called out to God, who was my only Hope, my only Help, my only Health. And He in His great compassion heard me. He reached down and healed me.

And as He had healed my body, so now, as He seemed to

enter into me, He healed my soul. I felt the holy presence of Christ within me. And what could be more logical? Why would He save my body, which is mortal and perishing, unless He also planned to save my soul, which is immortal and imperishable? Now He had accomplished both. . . .

My physical recovery was extremely rapid after this, all through the month of July 1978. Before long all my mental imaging was coming true: I *did* get out of that chair, I *did* take walks (first short ones, and then longer and longer, up to a mile!). I *did* start to ride my bicycle; I *did* drive my car!

All the while I continued thanking God so often and praising Him so much, that I pictured Him saying: "Oh, come on, Harry!" I kind of felt that He appreciated it though.

Friends were astounded to see me up and about and so active. My strength was increasing daily, and I began to gain back some of the weight I had lost. Finally, one day Bess said, "Har . . . you'd better cut back on the food. You're getting a little heavy . . . don't you think?"

It was true. I was eating everything that did not eat me first. I took another bite of my sandwich and then said, "Hey, Bess, remember when you were *screaming* at me to eat? Well . . . ?" Then I went back to munching my sandwich. Bess stood there with her hands on her hips. For once she was at a loss for words.

Oh! It was just great to be *alive!*

7

The Calling

"You did not choose me, but I chose you and appointed you that you should go and bear fruit and that your fruit should abide. . . ."

John 15:16 RSV

Two things started happening in the middle of July 1979. I started playing golf again, and I began taking chemotherapy. The golf was enjoyable; the chemotherapy practically did me in.

Three weeks after I was healed I was due to check in with my doctor. Dutifully I called him. "How are you feeling these days, Harry?" he asked.

"Great, doctor . . . wonderful."

"That's good. Harry, I want you to begin chemotherapy right away. Call Dr. Morgan over in Red Bank. He's expecting your call."

"But that's just it, Doctor," I replied, "I've been healed. I don't think I need any chemotherapy."

"Look, Harry, I'm glad you're feeling better, but I really think. . . ."

"Doc," I interrupted, "I've really changed! I have a lot of faith in God, and I know I've been healed. I'm eating again, taking walks—I'm all better!"

"Harry, keep that faith," he replied patiently. "It's wonderful, and I'm really delighted. But, really I'd like you to begin the chemotherapy. Now promise me you'll call Dr. Morgan. Okay?"

I felt slightly foolish and a little annoyed after our conversation. The doctor didn't believe me. *I* knew how I felt. "Bess, he wants me to take chemotherapy," I complained. "That stuff makes you sick, and I don't even need it!"

"Harry, I think you'd better listen to the doctor," she replied. "I think you should go."

Bess didn't really believe I was healed either. I'm sure she thought it was one of those temporary remissions and that the cancer would flare up again, although she never let on.

"But, Bess, I'm telling you I don't *need* it. I'm feeling fine," I protested.

"Well, I think you should go. Harry, it's at least one more thing we can do! Please. . . ."

"Okay . . . okay! I'll go! But it's under protest!" I warned.

I felt like a character in one of those movies who is unjustly accused of a crime. He's trying desperately to convince someone—anyone—that he's innocent, but nobody's buying it. And they're going to send him to jail or put him in the electric chair. I had a feeling the "chemo" was going to be almost as bad as the chair.

We made the appointment with Dr. Morgan, and a few days later drove over to his office. I was still feeling belligerent.

"I don't want to see this d______ doctor!" I snapped as we left the house. (The Lord hadn't yet cleaned up my vocabulary or softened my temper!) "Bess," I argued, "I don't think he's going to do that much for me anyway. Chemotherapy is not all that great from what I hear. It makes your hair fall out!"

"Well, at least you have nothing to worry about in *that* department," Bess quipped, glancing at my already bald head. "Let's just see what the man has to say!"

It was a lost cause. I climbed in on the passenger side and stared straight ahead. I could feel Bess looking at me, as she turned on the ignition. She was only doing what she thought best, but I wouldn't acknowledge her.

Dr. Morgan turned out to be bearded, short, cocky, and cold. He had my file open on the desk before him. "Mr. DeCamp, I've gone over your records. I . . . uh . . . I've also been in touch with Sloan-Kettering. Mr. DeCamp, after looking over your file, I think taking chemotherapy would be a waste of time."

Well, the man was honest at least. I glanced at Bess. She looked as if someone had slapped her hard. I felt as if I had been slapped too. I had been feeling so good, so healthy. And now this! He was saying I was so far gone that. . . .

"If you decide to take it," the doctor was saying, "I must tell you, that you have less than a 24 percent chance of recovering. Now, if you want to take it, it's entirely up to you." With that he sat back and drummed his fingers on my open file and looked off into space, waiting for my reply.

Again I looked at Bess. "Yes . . . let's try it," she said firmly.

A few days later we reported for my first treatment. When we entered the waiting room, I was shocked. I had a feeling of *déjà vu,* of having been through it all before. A roomful of zombies again. These people were as somber and haggard as living corpses. Some were in wheelchairs, some on crutches, some with no hair, and some with parts of their faces disfigured and bandaged. "What am I doing here?" I gasped to Bess.

"Now, Hon, just relax, and don't let them bother you!"

Bother me? These people were staring at me as if they were wondering what I was doing there. I was still pretty scrawny, a real sad sack, but I looked positively healthy by comparison. I wanted to run, but at the same time my heart went out to these poor souls. They were doomed—without hope or a future. *As I had been, short weeks before. . . .*

There was an interminable wait, punctuated by heart-rending screams emanating from behind closed doors. Finally, it was my turn. The room I was ushered into was stark. It had a small metal chest of drawers, half open and containing small bottles and vials. There were two chairs and an adjustable table.

I was asked to sit in a straight-backed chair. The nurse who was to administer the drugs talked pleasantly as she smacked the back of my hand to get the vein to pop up.

"Where do you live, Mr. DeCamp? Are you still working? . . . No? . . . What hospitals were you in? . . . Oh, yes? I know some nurses at Sloan-Kettering. Did you meet a small, dark pretty nurse named Sue? You *did!* Isn't she cute? I'll tell her you're coming here for treatments . . . Yes, I'll give her your regards. . . ."

All the while she chatted, she was filling a huge cylindrical plastic tube with red fluid. I was thinking with alarm, *I'll never be able to hold all that . . . and in a vein?*

The tube had a "reducer" attached to one end. From this reducer ran a long, narrow tube to which was attached a needle about the size of a darning needle. At the opposite end of this contraption was a plunger.

The needle was inserted in the vein and the red fluid was forced slowly into my system with the plunger. I could actually feel the cold, red liquid going into me and circulating through my blood stream. I was apprehensive: What would it do to me? I was about to find out.

My head and tongue got the first jolts. The tip of my tongue became numb, then the inside of my head seemed to be swelling; it felt very strange. My stomach got the next jolt; something hit it—plop! I became queasy, then nauseous, then *sick!*

The trip back home was a nightmare. Bess had to pull over to the side of the road several times to let me jump out and vomit. Once home, I dashed into the bathroom and heaved again. Then, every half hour, like clockwork, I was back—retching into the bowl. All the pretty colored chemicals they had so carefully pumped into me seemed to be emptying out in front of me. It was disgusting. To add to my utter misery was the knowledge that here was $204 worth of stuff going right into the sewer—and $40 of it was *mine!* When I had thrown up all the chemicals and thought there was nothing left, then I started heaving bile.

These chemotherapy treatments continued for twenty months! First I took them every three weeks, then every four weeks, finally every five weeks. For five days after each treatment, I couldn't eat; I would lose from five to eight pounds. All I could do was sit in my easy chair and be sick. All the great progress I had been making seemed to be totally undone. I was worried—not that the harsh treatments would bring the cancer back, but what else the strong chemicals might do to my body.

I know that doctors and medicine are good; they are given to us by a loving God for our well being. And I knew that those harsh treatments were being administered to me in good faith, in the hope that they would arrest and perhaps even cure my incurable cancer. How could the doctors know I had been healed by God? Or why, even if they had known, would they believe it? Science is the only healer in their belief system. So I just took it. I had to, to satisfy the doctors, to satisfy Bess. But by the third treatment they said, "We don't know what you are doing, but keep doing it. Your blood is completely changed."

After the five days, I would begin to return to normal. I would begin eating again and put back the pounds the treatment had melted off me. I would begin to walk again and to exercise.

During the stretches between my "chemo" treatments, I began taking my golf clubs out into our backyard on Hendrickson Place and practicing my swing. True, I didn't have much "oomph," thanks to the chemotherapy, but I was swinging, nevertheless.

I had a small group of friends who were willing to help me. They asked me to accompany them to the golf course. First it was nine holes, then thirteen, then eighteen—and I walked every step of the way, sweating and struggling—but

I did it! And because I was swinging the clubs easier, with less strength (and therefore less tension), I was actually hitting the ball better! I wish I had learned that much earlier in life—I would have been a better golfer!

In between the chemo, exercise, and golf, I started to pick up the pieces of my life by visiting old friends and business associates. It was then that I learned a disturbing fact: my friends and associates did not want to see me! They would make silly excuses not to see me, or if they found themselves suddenly face to face with me, they would literally back off—cringe almost—in an effort not to touch me. In their ill-concealed panic, there was minimal finesse, much less kindness. It was all so clumsily obvious; it was shocking and hurt me deeply.

I remember in particular a retirement party for a former business associate to which I had been invited.

"How ya doing, Harry!" an old friend said, as I walked in. But as I proffered my hand, he looked over my head and called out, "Hey, Charlie!" and maneuvered away more skillfully than Wilt Chamberlain on the basketball court. It was as if he had said, "Harry, we were friends once, but don't get near me now!"

I stood there for an instant, feeling a flush of anger. Then, lowering my hand, I turned toward the bar.

"Harry," my host called out with a joviality that seemed forced. "You're looking great, boy!" he lied enthusiastically. "Scotch and water, right?"

"Right."

There was no tinkle of ice cubes falling into a glass, even though drinks were being served in tumblers. I stared in stunned disbelief as he handed me my drink *in a paper cup!* He was still wearing that forced smile, though small beads of sweat were suddenly on his brow. I stared at the man for a long moment. In the old days I think I would have thrown the drink in his face for the insult, but the Lord was working a change in my heart. Instead, I put that paper cup down and turned and pushed my way through the laughing crowd toward the door.

To most of my former friends and associates I was a contagious disease walking around.

I thank the good Lord for my golfing buddies and the guys down at the boat club. It's really true, you know; you will never know who your true friends are until something like cancer hits you.

I had been a member of the Long Branch Ice-Boat and Yacht Club for about twenty years. I was one of the "social" members, which meant I didn't own a boat. (To me the word *boat* is synonymous with a hole in the water, into which you pour money!) Anyway, now that I was getting stronger and stronger, I would venture down to the club, which is located on Renwick Place in Long Branch, right on the Shrewsbury River. (We call it our "river-front property.") Soon I was going down daily, as regularly as I used to go to work—that is, when I wasn't sick as a dog from the chemotherapy.

Most of the boat club members are regular guys, blue-collar workers or middle-management executives. A nicer, more unpretentious group of guys you could never meet. Hanging out with them was the best post-cancer therapy I could have had. They openly joked with me about the "Big C" and never gave me a bit of sympathy. They treated me as though there was nothing wrong with me; I was just one of the gang.

This was the code at the boat club. I remember once, one of the guys tripped on a rock and fractured his ankle, just as he was coming in for lunch. The other guys were already eating. They paused long enough to pick him up, lay him on a spare table, and pack his ankle with ice, and then they went back to their beer and cold cuts. They figured he had only twisted his ankle.

All the time the guy is lying on the table, yelling bloody murder. "Ah, be quiet and stop your bellyaching!" somebody said.

"Yeah, pipe down and let us finish our lunch in peace, for crying out loud!" somebody else chimed in. So he clowned along with them, but the pain wouldn't let up. So finally, the guys saw he was serious and called the ambulance. By the time it arrived, they were really concerned. But, again, they wouldn't show *him* they were.

I remember my first day back at the boat club. Usually, they'd just be sitting around drinking coffee, and they'd have all the problems of the world solved by lunchtime. (And if the President of the United States were to call on any given day, these guys would tell him what to do about the national *and* the international situations.) But on this particular day, they were all outside, taking a boat off the blocks.

"Come on, Har!" my friend Mike DeLisa said gruffly, "get off your duff and help us!" But as soon as I positioned myself to lift, two guys quickly moved alongside me to take the weight. God bless those guys! They weren't about to let me *really* do any heavy work. They were just wise enough to let me be part of things again. They may have been all sympathy behind my back—and I'm sure they were. But they never once let on. And that was the best medicine I could have had.

Christmas 1978 came. What a world of difference between this happy celebration and the sad, strained one of the previous year. I was really enjoying the holiday, instead of sweating out the days before surgery. *And I was free of cancer!* How grateful I was to God for His goodness! When I heard choirs singing, "Joy to the world, the Lord is come . . ." I really felt it, for the first time.

If Jesus hadn't been born all those long centuries ago, I would never have known His power and love. If Jesus hadn't been born, I would never have dared to pray in faith as I lay dying. If Jesus hadn't been born, I would never have known His healing touch. If Jesus hadn't been born, I would have missed the peace and the joy and the fellowship that knowing Him has given me.

I thought of how I had ignored Him all those years of my life before my cancer; I almost died, not knowing Him. *If Jesus hadn't been born. . . .* The thought was absolutely frightening, unthinkable.

So that Christmas of 1978, for the first time in my 68 years, I experienced the real meaning and joy of the holiday. And that meaning is Jesus Christ. Because of Him, I had a New Year and a new life to live.

Right after I was healed, I had promised God that because He had healed me, I would shout His praises from the

it, God was about to bring

ı.

ıotice from the Firestone
tires, which already had
recalled because of a de-
g to get a brand-new set of
me to bring my car to the

ɔver to the garage. When I
ıe said, "Okay, leave your
ı can wait in here," and he
ren rooms all garages and
cold, empty, and smelling
d a "sofa" which was the
ɔor and shoved up against

ndant ushered in a well-
hite hair. The man stood
up and down. He looked

wait," I said. "They're
you come over and sit

y at the car seat, but care-
pcoat, to avoid the dirty
floor, he sat down beside me.

We chatted about the raw March weather a bit, and then I said, "You appear to be a salesman. Are you?"

"I suppose I am, in a way," he replied.

"What kind of sales?" I asked, adding, "I used to sell insurance."

"Well, I'm actually a minister," he said.

"Oh," I laughed, "you sell *God!*"

"Yes . . . yes, I do, as a matter of fact!" he replied with a grin. Then he told me he was affiliated with the Ocean Grove (New Jersey) Auditorium as the program director. His name was the Reverend Floyd George.

I told him I had been in Ocean Grove and the auditorium, but I had never been to any of the religious services held there. Ocean Grove was founded as a strict religious community, and only recent court decisions had forced the town fathers to allow motor vehicle traffic on Sundays. Ocean Grove has remained something of an anachronism among the bustling, commercially-oriented New Jersey shore communities.

"You have Norman Vincent Peale over there sometimes, don't you?" I asked. I don't know why I mentioned Dr. Peale just then; the name popped into my head. I knew he was a practitioner of positive thinking.

"Why, yes, we do," replied Dr. George. "As a matter of fact, we're going to have Dr. Peale down to speak on Labor Day."

"Gee! I'd love to hear him speak some time," I said.

"Would you like to meet him?" he asked.

"I'd love to!" I replied, perking up.

"Tell you what," he said. "On Labor Day Sunday, if you'll come over to the auditorium—to the back door—oh, say about 6:45 P.M., I'll see if I can get you an introduction to Dr. Peale. Okay? By the way," he added, "why are you so interested in Norman Peale?"

"I think his ideas are great—positive thinking, the power of God within us, and all that."

"Why do you think it's so great?" he asked, studying me intently.

"I had a little problem," I replied, pretending to study the zipper on my jacket.

"Oh, what was that?"

"I . . . uh . . . had cancer," I replied. "And . . . uh . . . through faith and prayer and positive thinking, I was healed." I felt a small lump in my throat, remembering. I looked at him to see his reaction.

He was looking at me steadily. "Would you care to elaborate on that?" he asked.

So, while we waited for my tires to be changed, I told the minister my story. When I had finished, he looked at me for a moment and then said, "Harry, that was a terrific story!"

Just then the attendant came in and told me my car was ready. "Well," I said, standing and offering my hand, "it's been nice meeting you."

"Nice meeting you, Harry," he replied, shaking my hand. "I wish you well. . . ."

I got my car and drove home. There I mentioned my meeting Dr. George to Bess, and the possibility that I might get to meet Norman Vincent Peale. In a few days I had forgotten all about it.

The following month, a woman reporter from *The Asbury Park Press* came out to the house to ask me about West Long Branch. I was a senior ex-councilman, and was fairly well versed in the history of our town. After she had interviewed me, Bess invited her to stay for coffee. The two women fell into conversation, and the reporter mentioned with a sigh that her favorite aunt had just learned she had cancer. Of course the woman's entire family was distraught. "We know just how you feel!" Bess said sympathetically, patting her arm. "Harry had cancer, you know. And he's been healed, haven't you, Har?"

"Is that so?" the reporter said, perking up. "Uh . . . Mr. DeCamp, would you care to tell me about it?"

So I told her the whole story. After I had finished she said, "I'd like to tell my editor about this. I think I'd like to come back and talk to you again, do a story. How . . . how would you feel about that?" she asked, looking first at me, then at Bess.

"It would be just fine," I replied, "no problem."

Three weeks later, in early May, she was back with a photographer. We went over the story once more.

The following Sunday, the story of my healing appeared on the first page of the Panorama feature section, with a picture of Bess and me. They gave the story big play—a quarter of a page.

A few days later, I received a letter from Dr. George, which read:

> Dear Harry:
>
> You may recall our meeting in March when we were at the Firestone garage to get new tires. I read your story in the Press the other day. Would you be interested in appearing on the program with Dr. Peale on Labor Day, to bear witness to the wonderful thing the Lord has done for you?
>
> Your testimony needn't be long; we think five minutes would be sufficient. Will you give me a call . . . ?

Excitedly, I read the letter to Bess. "Say, what does 'bear witness' mean, Hon?" I asked her.

"It just means you get up and tell your story for God, Har."

I could hardly believe it. I mean, first the minister invited me to the back door of the Ocean Grove Auditorium, to *maybe* get a quick introduction to the famous Dr. Norman Vincent Peale. Now, all of a sudden, I was going to be on the stage with him! On the same program! *Speaking!* It was incredible!

Well, I was so flattered by that invitation and so proud that I told everybody and his uncle. I made the mistake of telling the guys at the boat club. They began to rib me mercilessly.

They cut a funny story out of the paper and passed it all around:

It seems that there was a preacher who took a sabbatical and toured the Bible Belt, sermonizing on the evils of fast living, drink, and wild women. And he took along a fellow, by the name of Clyde, who happened to be the town drunk. Clyde would be onstage during the preacher's sermon, drunk as a skunk. And as old Clyde sat there picking his nose, burping, and falling off his chair, the preacher would be singling him out as a horrible example of the kind of life he was talking about.

Well, the guys had crossed Clyde's name out, throughout the story, and had carefully written in "Harry DeCamp." And when it got to me, they included a letter stating that poor Clyde had died, and asking me if I was looking for old Clyde's job! Next, they started kidding me about *being* Clyde and Dr. Peale being the preacher! Finally, they nicknamed me Clyde. "Hey, Clyde!" they'd say, "won't be long now! Labor Day's coming up. Hey, old Clyde's going to be on the stage with Norman Vincent Peale. Did you know *that?*"

It was all in good fun. But I was really getting nervous, as September approached. I had carefully written out my story in longhand, and had practiced it while walking on the beach. It was much, much too long, so I worked at cutting it down to four minutes. When I had it trimmed, I committed it to memory. I was determined to be prepared.

The big day arrived, Labor Day Sunday, 1979. I hadn't slept a wink the night before, and was nervous as a cat, as we drove over to Ocean Grove. There was my brother George, my sister Hannah, and our good friends Harry and Zeta Rehm. Judy, Rick, and the kids were on vacation and so they missed Pop Pop's big night.

I wore a dignified dark suit. When we got there, Bess fussed with my tie and said, "Now, Har, don't be nervous!

Just go out there and tell them the story as it happened."

Bess, Harry, and Zeta went into the auditorium, and met George and Hannah, who had arrived earlier. I went to the back door and told the attendant who I was. "Follow me, please, Mr. DeCamp," he said, conducting me to an anteroom behind the stage. Dr. George and a number of people were there, including Dr. and Mrs. Peale. After hurrying over to shake my hand, Dr. George introduced me to the Peales.

Dr. Peale turned out to be a jovial, affable man, who tried to make me feel at ease. I'm a big man, and I towered over him physically, but just being in the presence of the much celebrated preacher made me feel, well . . . *miniscule.*

"Let's take a picture of Harry with Dr. Peale," Mr. George suggested to a photographer. We all moved to the back steps while the camera clicked away. After this, Dr. Peale was surrounded by admirers and staff members, so I found myself suddenly alone and not quite sure what to do with myself.

Mrs. Peale gave me a warm smile that told me she understood how I was feeling. She was a kindly woman with clear, intelligent eyes.

"What are you going to talk about, Mr. DeCamp?" she inquired pleasantly.

"About my healing from cancer."

"Oh, yes . . ." she replied in an interested but almost matter-of-fact way. "We've heard of cases like yours before." Mrs. Peale seemed totally at home with the idea that I had experienced a miraculous healing. And here I was thinking that nobody really believed it but *me!* I began to relax.

"Let's go, everyone!" Dr. George was saying. I followed Dr. and Mrs. Peale out onto the stage. There were four guest chairs. As I took my seat I was half conscious of the buzzing of the congregation. Up behind us was a large choir of pleasant-faced people in robes.

Crowds have never fazed me; I had played sports as a young man and so I was used to performing in front of large groups. But when I raised my eyes, I almost fell out of my chair. Before me was a sea of faces! The crowd overflowed the auditorium. The large balcony was jammed to capacity. *There were eight thousand people in that room, and all of them were waiting for me to talk!* (Well, they were waiting for *Dr. Peale* to talk. Me, they were going to have to put up with!)

After the initial surprise of seeing the size of the gathering, I settled down, though I was still awestruck at being on the same stage with Dr. Peale.

Dr. George got up and made some opening remarks. Then he introduced Dr. and Mrs. Peale. There was a roar of applause.

"We also have a fellow with us today, Harry DeCamp, of West Long Branch. I met Harry a few months back when we went to have our tires changed during the Firestone tire recall. Harry has a rather appealing story. I'd like you to hear it." With that he turned and nodded to me.

I got up and walked to the podium.

"In April 1976, it was found that I had cancer of the bladder . . ." I began. Then it hit me. First I felt it in my stomach, then it seemed to grab me by the throat. I can't explain exactly what it was, but the minute I began to tell my story, my composure deserted me. The experience of having cancer all came rushing back; I was reliving every moment of it, it seemed! I choked up; my legs felt weak. Then I began to cry.

I struggled on, my eyes on the podium, which I could no longer see, so blurred was my sight by the tears.

"From April 1976 . . . until December 1977 . . . I was in and . . . out . . . of the hospital every . . . three months, having the can . . . cancer burned off. . . ." By now I was sobbing audibly.

Oh, dear God, help me get through this! I prayed in my mind, as haltingly, agonizingly, I told my story, stammering it out in bits and pieces. *I have to let them know!* I pleaded inwardly, *I must!*

I don't really know how long it took, but my talk which was to have lasted five minutes at the most, must have stretched to at least twenty minutes. That vast crowd seemed to be holding its collective breath. The only sound in the entire hall was the sound of my sobbing.

I finished, and without looking up, turned and walked back to my seat. I was oblivious to any reaction. The important thing was that I had done it. I had told my story. It was only in that moment that I realized what had just happened: I had told God I would shout His praises from the housetops, and He had just taken me up on it! *This is God, holding you to your promise,* a voice seemed to whisper.

My friends, let me warn you—never make a promise to God unless you are prepared to fulfill it. That thought ran over and over in my mind as I sat there.

I looked up to see Dr. Peale standing over me. In a soft voice he said, "Harry, that is the most moving testimony I have ever heard in my life!"

Then he walked to the podium and said something to the crowd that I'll never forget. "How in the world do you follow a fellow like *that?*" Then during his sermon (which, ironically, was about the town drunk back in his birthplace in Ohio), Dr. Peale kept referring to my story. What a thrill it had been, just to meet a man of the stature of Norman Vincent Peale; and now *this!* I felt touched, moved, humbled by it all. *God was using me, a small-town man, a nobody to spread His word!*

After Dr. Peale's sermon, there was a hymn and then the benediction. Then the service was over.

Afterwards, I went outside with Bess and the others. It was warm, so I removed my jacket and loosened my tie. A woman rushed up to me. "Mr. DeCamp!" she exclaimed, "that was so *touching!* Just wonderful! God bless you!" And with that she kissed me on the cheek. I was startled.

Next, two men came up. "Harry DeCamp? That was a

terrific testimony!" one of them said, pumping my hand. Other people were converging on me. . . .

Later, on the way home, I felt a sense of happy relief. "I didn't think you'd get through it, Har," Bess was saying. "I was crying, and Hannah was crying, too!" I was surprised but my family and friends took the entire thing seriously. There was no ribbing. No "Clyde" jokes.

Later, as I sat in the quiet of our living room, I thought of how I—an irreligious man—had been placed before eight thousand religious people, in a temple of God. I had met and participated with the internationally-known Dr. Norman Vincent Peale in presenting to this group of Christians the truth that God lives and acts today. *It was mind boggling!* "Wow, God, You sure are something!" I mused.

The following day, the local papers carried the picture of Dr. Peale and me shaking hands on the back steps of the auditorium. It was heady stuff for an everyday guy like me. My feet remained airborne for several days—even with Bess trying to let the air out of my balloon by saying such things as, "Oh, come now, Harry! Norman Vincent Peale has probably forgotten your name already. He meets captains of industry, heads of state, world figures. What makes you think he'd remember you?"

"I guess you're right, Hon," I sighed. "But *I* sure will remember *him!* Imagine me on the same program . . . !"

Well, Dr. Peale did remember! He sent me a personal letter, about a week after Ocean Grove. It was complimentary and what's more, was personally signed by him! The letter even carried his home address!

Proudly, I showed the letter to Bess, Rick, Judy, and the grandkids. I thought I might get a nice frame for it. I must admit, it was kind of hard settling back down to my regular routine of raking the leaves and taking the garbage out, after Ocean Grove. It had been a rare, mountaintop experience, but now it was time to get back to real life. I had been a weekend celebrity, but now I was just your ordinary Joe, down the street. I consoled myself that I had Dr. Peale's letter as a memento; and more important, I had kept my promise to God.

About two weeks passed, and then I was surprised one sunny afternoon by a phone call. A man introduced himself as Bill Boetcker, of some group called the Foundation for Christian Living, located in Pawling, New York. The foundation (or FCL, as he called it) had been started by Dr. and Mrs. Peale, he explained. The FCL published Dr. Peale's sermons and articles. They also held week-long seminars for ministers and their wives, to help recharge spiritual batteries. Mr. Boetcker told me the seminar weekend was coming up and that some two hundred fifty clergy and their wives would be in attendance, some of them from as far away as England.

"Mr. DeCamp," Boetcker said, "we're wondering if you would like to be our guest that weekend, to share your story with these ministers. Of course, we'd like Mrs. DeCamp to come along too, if she'd like." I readily agreed.

"What do you think of that, Hon?" I asked Bess, after I had filled her in on the invitation.

"What'll we do? Will you be the only speaker?" she asked, already nervous about the prospect.

"Well, we'll soon find out, won't we?" I said, grinning. Then I added, "Boy oh boy, Bess!"

"What . . . ? And *stop* grinning like that!"

"And *you* said Norman Vincent Peale would forget!"

So it was that we made the first of what were to be many trips over the next four years to Pawling and the Foundation for Christian Living. They put us up at a motel on Friday night. That evening we had dinner at the foundation meeting place, Short Hills (a YMCA facility), located at a beautiful site in Pawling. We were seated at Dr. and Mrs. Peale's table, along with others. Dr. Peale seemed so down to earth and "regular" for a man of his position. There wasn't a pretentious bone in his body.

The next morning, just before the seminar at which I was

to speak, I prayed, asking God to be with me, to help me. I was just an ordinary man from West Long Branch who had been thrust in among a group of educated, powerful church leaders—world movers! "I can't do it without You, God!" I prayed.

There were two other speakers on the program with me: a Homer Surbeck, a distinguished Wall Street attorney, and Gus Thomes, a mortician from Pawling. Both men turned out to be excellent speakers with powerful testimonies of how God had touched their lives. Then it was my turn.

"How in the world do you follow two such silver-tongued orators?" I began. "I must tell you I am not a public speaker, I am not a theologian, nor do I belong to any organized church group. Which brings up the obvious question: What am I doing here?"

There was a burst of nervous laughter from the audience.

"I am here," I continued, "because I made a promise to God, that when He healed me of cancer, I would shout His praises from the housetops. I am here to keep that promise.

"In April 1976, it was found that I had cancer of the bladder. . . ." Then it hit me again! I totally lost my composure, as I began to relive the ordeal, the triumph of my fight against cancer. Sobbing, choking, stumbling, I told my story. . . . How could it have happened *again?* Just when I thought I had everything under control!

In the four years since then, I have returned to the FCL at least ten times. And every time I begin to speak, the same thing always happens. I tell my story haltingly, brokenly, with tears. Strangely, just prior to approaching the podium, I am calm and totally confident. Repeated appearances have increased sureness. Yet, the minute I begin to speak, the tears and the sobbing begin.

Why this should be, I have no idea. In a way, maybe this vulnerability is the price a man has to pay when God reaches down to touch him in a miraculous way. I'm not sure. I suspect that *this is the way God wants my story told, since I can tell it no other way.*

If I had my druthers, I'd want to tell my story smoothly, and if not with polished phrases, at least without tears. It's hard to believe, but four years of practice have not polished my delivery one whit. I know now what Paul felt when he wrote to the Corinthian Christians:

> When I came to you, brethren, I did not come proclaiming to you the testimony of God in lofty words or wisdom. For I decided to know nothing among you except Jesus Christ and him crucified. And I was with you in weakness and in much fear and trembling; and my speech and my message were not in plausible words of wisdom, but in demonstration of the Spirit and power, that your faith might not rest in the wisdom of men but in the power of God.
>
> 1 Corinthians 2:1–5 RSV

Our Christian faith is full of paradoxes; many of God's methods are just the opposite of the way the world would expect them to be. We would have Christ born in a palace, but God chose a manger; we would choose for His followers the richest, most educated, and religious men of His time, but God called a bunch of nobodies, among them a fisherman, a rascally tax collector, and a prostitute. Jesus Himself never said, "I am the powerful king," but He did say, "I am the Good Shepherd."

In a given situation if we want to figure out what God would do, perhaps we should decide what *we* would do and then be almost sure that God would do the opposite thing. Constantly throughout history, God has used the weakest, the lowliest, the most obscure and unlettered by the world's standards to proclaim His message.

Don't mistake me; the church needs its brilliant preachers like the Billy Grahams and the Norman Vincent Peales. But in certain instances polish, wit, and erudition could weaken or distract from a special point He wants to make. That is why God sometimes uses a man like me. In spite of my limitations, my weakness (and perhaps *because* of them), His power comes through.

Closely connected with this, I think, is the fact that Harry DeCamp is a plain Joe, the guy down the street. People can relate to that.

Suppose God only healed presidents, stockbrokers, and big-league ballplayers. People would think, "Well, I'm not as important as that man. God wouldn't have the time or interest to heal a *nobody* like me."

My friends, that is exactly why He healed a *nobody* like Harry DeCamp—so the rest of you *nobodies* can't say that! It's so that (to quote Paul again) ". . . your faith might not rest in the wisdom of men but in the power of God" (1 Corinthians 2:5).

People can clearly see that I'm an ordinary man. They say, "Well, if God healed him, why not me? I'm just as good as he is." Because Harry DeCamp is an ordinary man, other ordinary people can suddenly catch the vision that healing—even healing from cancer—is possible for them, too!

That's really quite wonderful when you think about it. The Lord knew all this in advance, and He chose His instrument accordingly. That's pretty humbling, and a bit frightening. You know He's singled you out. It's a grave responsibility. It puts you on your guard against pride. You know God is watching you.

At any rate, that first time at the Foundation for Christian Living, I got through my talk again. Suddenly the entire room was on its feet, giving me a standing ovation! I felt so humbled; the tears started all over again.

Then Dr. Peale got up, and with his booming voice and no-nonsense delivery said, "Wasn't that a moving speech? (Applause.) How would you like to follow that man on a program? (Pause.) I followed him on the stage at Ocean Grove last month, and I never felt so *inferior* in my life! (Uproarious laughter.)"

* * *

Later, during coffee break, people rushed up to me to shake my hand, or kiss my cheek or hug me. "Very touching! . . ." "My brother has cancer; I'm going to tell him about your experience. . . ." "Thank you for sharing that with us!"

One lady approached me timidly and said, "I would like very much to touch you."

Kind of silly, I thought, but I extended my hand, and she touched my sleeve lightly. It made me feel uneasy. I was to find, to my dismay, that some people mistakenly think that you are some kind of saint to have experienced what I've experienced. They put you on a pedestal. They treat you almost as if you were Christ! And that's a sin.

What they think will happen when they touch me, I don't know. No matter how many times I tell them that God, through Jesus Christ, is the only Healer, and that God healed an ordinary man when He healed Harry DeCamp, a few people still insist on getting it all mixed up.

Another sad thing is to see the skeptics, particularly among the clergy. Our whole society, including the church, has been so brainwashed by scientific materialism, that we cannot believe that God will (or even *can*) heal a man of cancer, after the doctors have given up on him.

"What medication are you on now?" one minister asked, not long ago.

"I'm not on any medication now," I replied. "I've been healed. The only thing I am on is big doses of God—hourly."

He looked at me peculiarly, as if he didn't quite believe it.

Happily, many clergymen and their wives come up after the FCL meetings and tell me that my testimony has restored their faith in the Bible. Suddenly the healing miracles of Jesus, and all the other miracles in Scripture that they had been taught to regard as myths, not to be taken literally, seem possible to them, because a real miracle happened to me, a twentieth-century man. Isn't that something?

When they ask me why some people are healed and not

others, I tell them I don't know. Mel, George, Vince, Jim, and I all had cancer at the same time. They weren't religious and neither was I. They were men just like me, no better and no worse. Yet they all died and I lived. Why God ordained this I do not know. The realization leaves me awestruck, humbled. *Dumbfounded.*

I tell people, "If everyone had gold, then it would have no value, would it? Likewise, if everyone were always healed, then healings would not be miraculous, would they?" (Not to mention the fact that the world would be so crowded that we'd all be standing on one another's heads!)

After that initial appearance at the Foundation for Christian Living, Dr. Peale suggested my story to *Guideposts* magazine. (Yes, it turned out that the very magazine that put me onto this whole faith business is published by my now good friend, Dr. Peale! A coincidence? I think not.)

My experience appeared as the cover story in the May 1980 issue of the magazine, under the title, "Believe, Believe, Believe." The response was so overwhelming that *Guidepost*s published a follow-up story in the January 1981 issue under the title, "After the Miracle."

After all this attention and publicity, as you might expect, Bess says every once in a while, "Now, Har, don't go getting a swelled head!"

Not much danger of that. The minute you ride away from the heady atmosphere of one of the Foundation for Christian Living weekends—boom! You come right back down into the real world. The next day I'm raking those leaves, taking the garbage out, and trying to figure out how we're going to pay the heating oil bill—just like folks everywhere. It really is kind of hard, coming down off the mountain top, but you have to. It keeps your feet planted firmly on the ground and your priorities straight. God is the Boss, and Harry DeCamp is the servant.

So you see, Harry is no different from anyone else—he's no different from you—except that God gave him the gift of faith to believe he could be healed of terminal cancer. But even healing has its limitations, wonderful as it is. I'm 72 now, and have exceeded the biblical threescore and ten, but I know that even though God spared my life in 1976, I have to die sometime. Conceivably, I could step off the curb tomorrow and get hit by a truck. (Though I really don't think God will let it happen!)

Contrary to what you might think, when the Lord touches you, He doesn't automatically make you perfect in body, mind, and soul. I have to grow and struggle with my faith, my honest doubts, my human weaknesses. I still argue with my wife and my daughter . . . and occasionally yell at my grandchildren.

Even more important than my physical healing, is the wonderful fact that the Lord saved my soul at the same time. I'm not trying to sound pious. But what good would it do for the Lord to heal the body of a man already in late middle age if He weren't going to do anything about his spiritual condition? Physical healing was only a prelude to a deeper healing that will last for eternity.

Today, I'm a changed man in many ways. Take forgiveness. I used to hate my enemies—people who had crossed me in business or politics. I carried grudges and would not have been sorry to see an enemy go bankrupt or lose his health. But Christ commands me in His Word to "Love your enemies, bless them that curse you, do good to them that hate you, and pray for them who despitefully use you, and persecute you" (Matthew 5:44).

Now, the Lord helps me to pray for my former enemies; I ask Him to help them in their businesses and to bless their lives. He didn't say it would be easy to do this, and it isn't, but He gives me the grace to do it.

Another change is that I've stopped drinking. It didn't happen all at once. After I was healed, I continued to drink socially. I read in the Bible where Jesus turned water into wine—presumably for people to enjoy—so I didn't see anything wrong with it.

I was carrying out my promise to God to shout His praises from the housetops, because He had healed me; but I felt over a period of time that I wanted to do something more to show Him my gratitude. I wanted to make a sacrifice of some kind. And I decided it would be social drinking. It was the least I could do after His great goodness to me.

It was hard to stop, but not all that hard. And I felt good about it. Twice after I made my decision, I slipped and decided to cheat a little. (That will show you what a strong, "perfect" guy Harry DeCamp is!) Curiously, both times I tried it, when I raised the glass to my lips, I almost had to spit the stuff out. It tasted horrible!

Speaking of miracles—God had also taken away my taste for liquor.

8

The Messenger

"Then I said, 'Ah, Lord God! Behold, I do not know how to speak, for I am only a youth.' But the Lord said to me, 'Do not say, "I am only a youth"; for to all to whom I send you you shall go, and whatever I command you you shall speak. . . .' "

Jeremiah 1:6, 7 RSV

When I promised God I would shout His praises from the housetops for healing me of cancer, I meant it. But I had no idea of how I would do it. But *He* did. My talks at the Foundation for Christian Living seminars were one "housetop." Ocean Grove was another. Stories in the local press were a third. My two stories in *Guideposts* magazine, however, were probably the highest "housetops" the Lord gave me, from which to shout His praises.

Guideposts, which was founded by Dr. Peale and the late Lowell Thomas over thirty-seven years ago, is the world's most popular inter-faith magazine. The secret of this little magazine's success is that it does not deal in doctrine or theology. It focuses instead on the faith experiences of ordinary people from all walks of life—people like me, who are touched by God and are willing to share what happened to them with others. It does not moralize, proselytize, or theologize, but it does gently point confused, hurting people in the direction of God. *Guideposts* seemed to me to be the perfect vehicle for the story of a nonreligious type like me. Though I didn't know it at the time, the magazine has a pass-along readership of *almost 15 million people a month!* A high housetop indeed!

My picture appeared on the cover of the May 1980 issue, with a blurb: "One word changed everything for me." I was photographed wearing a cheerful red shirt and a contented smile, my arms folded across my chest. I looked the picture of health—which in fact I was.

Within a week of publication, letters and phone calls began pouring into our home. It seemed that everyone was trying to find God, and they thought I had His address and unlisted number.

The calls and letters came (and still come) from desperate people of all races and faiths and all walks of life—from whites, blacks, Hispanics, East Indians. Most of them are sick (many with cancer) or they have relatives who are gravely ill. All of them plead for simple answers about God and faith. They don't want to hear theological abstractions; they *want* and *need* answers they can cope with and understand.

They would call me (and still do) at all hours of the day and night—a 3 A.M. phone call is nothing unusual. Am I annoyed? Not a bit. I am happy to help in whatever way I can. In fact, when I get a call in the middle of the night, I feel kind of like a doctor; that call from a needy person becomes my priority, sleep is not.

I honestly believe that is why I am still here on this earth, to extend a friendly hand to sick, frightened, confused people, to tell them a little about the wonderful God we have, who wants them happy and well. Though it isn't much, I feel it is what God wants me to be doing. It is my work.

Bess feels the same way. If I'm not home when a call comes, she talks to the caller; she is wonderfully sympathetic and warm—especially to the wives of cancer victims.

She always tells them at what time to call back so they can talk to me.

What do I tell people when they ask me where they can find this wonderful God? My reply is always the same: "You will find Him in your heart and in your mind." And I remind them that Jesus Himself said, "The kingdom of God is within you" (Luke 17:21).

I like quoting the words of Christ to them. People always want to argue with me; they can't very well argue with *Him.* When they ask me, "How can I be sure God *wants* me healed?" I usually reply by quoting the Lord's Prayer, "Thy kingdom come. Thy will be done in earth, as it is in heaven." I tell them, "Jesus Christ Himself spoke those lines, gave them to us. And what do they really say? Well, we know that there is no sorrow or sickness in heaven. (There certainly isn't any cancer!) And if Jesus said, 'Thy will be done in earth *as* it is in heaven,' then that means that God's perfect will is that you be as happy and whole here on earth *as you would be in heaven,* where all is perfect."

And if they want to argue about that, I tell them that *I* didn't make that up; if they want to doubt the Lord's word, that's up to them.

One of the most touching encounters I had was the night, shortly after my first story appeared in *Guideposts*, when I received a long-distance call from Minnesota.

"Mr. DeCamp? I . . . I'm calling from my wife's hospital room at the Mayo Clinic," said the man at the other end in a husky voice. "Mr. DeCamp, the doctors have just told us that she has terminal cancer. No chance, they say. Could you . . . please talk to my wife? Maybe give her a little hope . . . ?"

I was so touched by their need that I could have cried. I told that man I would indeed speak to his wife. She came on the line, scared and crushed, because she had just been given the sentence of death. "Look . . . I know how you feel," I began, inwardly asking for the right words. "I know, because I've been there myself."

"Mr. DeCamp, I . . . I just can't believe it; it's like an awful dream. I'm so *scared!*" Her voice broke.

"Listen to me carefully," I said to the woman (whom I'll call Peggy Carlson, though that isn't her real name), *"I believe that God doesn't want you to die!* God wants you healthy and strong. Do you think you can believe this, too?"

"Yes . . . I think so! I *want* to so much!" she whispered.

"Good, Peggy! Now your job is to really desire health. And then you've got to affirm it, visualize it, *burn* it into your heart and subconscious mind. When you do this, you'll be in tune with God. You will be allowing His will—His healing power—to work through you.

"Peggy, do you recall how Jesus talked about having faith only as big as a tiny mustard seed? How that small amount of faith could move *mountains?* Well, it works! It did for me and my case was considered hopeless! Listen, I *know* it can work for you too!"

"Oh, do you really think so? Do you . . . ?" For the first time, there was something like hope in her voice.

"*Yes,* I do! Jesus said, 'Seek, and ye shall find'—but *you,* Peggy Carlson, have to do the seeking. Let me tell you, the prize is well worth it. It's your *life.*"

Peggy Carlson cried a little and thanked me. She said she would try to put faith into practice. I promised to follow up with a letter, which I did. Her husband then wrote back, thanking me. He said Peggy was reading and rereading my article in *Guideposts* and was really trying to put the positive principles of healing to work against her cancer.

Another caller (one of my favorites) was a Texan who told me that he too had been healed of cancer through prayer and faith. Pete called regularly for a while. He always began his conversation with a delightfully drawled, "How doin', Har?" Both he and his wife stopped off to have dinner with Bess and me on their way to a vacation in Germany to see the Passion Play.

One day a woman called to talk about her wayward son—at least she considered him wayward, because he was not doing what she wanted him to do. I was a bit dubious about the call. "Will you ask your prayer group to pray about my son?" she asked.

"I'm sorry, but I don't belong to a prayer group," I replied.

"You *don't?*" She was more than a bit shocked at this. "Well . . . then will you ask your church to pray about this?"

"Madam, I'm afraid I don't yet belong to a church either."

"You *don't* belong to a *church* and you say *God* healed you of *cancer!*" The woman was absolutely indignant.

"If I understand the Bible correctly," I replied, "Jesus said he came to minister to sinners. I am a sinner. I think you'll find that in Matthew, the ninth chapter, thirteenth verse. . . ."

Why do people think a man has to be "good" before God will help him? (Just how good is "good"?) That kind of thinking comes, I suspect, from a self-righteous spirit. It certainly has nothing to do with biblical Christianity.

One day, I had an unusual call from a woman who was distraught because her beloved dog was dying of cancer. I know some people would think that praying for a pet is inappropriate when so many human beings are in need. But I encouraged this woman to image her dog's healing. I reminded her that Jesus said, "Are not two sparrows sold for a penny? And not one of them will fall to the ground without your Father's will" (Matthew 10:29 RSV). Jesus seems to be saying that not even a little bird—or a dog—is beyond God's interest or care.

The woman thanked me and said she would try to put faith and imaging to work. Two weeks later, she wrote to say her veterinarian had found that the animal's cancer had totally disappeared! She was ecstatic with joy. What's more, because God had healed her pet, she was returning to church. She signed her letter, "A skeptic no more."

It is such a joy and pleasure to share my faith with people

in this way. Sitting on our sunny porch at the table, with Bess bustling nearby in the kitchen, the letters simply flow out of me, some of them seven, eight . . . ten pages long. I write people essentially the same message I gave Mrs. Peggy Carlson on the phone—that I know what they are suffering and they have to stop believing they are automatically going to die from cancer. To a woman in Inverness, Florida, I wrote:

"We are so brainwashed by the media, that the very word 'cancer' strikes total fear into us. We immediately think we are going to die. *Wrong!* If we persist with that thought, however, God listens and believes that the negative thought is our prayer, and He gives us what we are thinking—which is Death.

"Now, if we believe God-power is stronger than Cancer-power, and we maintain the thought that we are going to *live*—God hears and knows *that* is our prayer. He answers by giving us Life.

"The use of imagery is very potent; not only in helping people change their feelings, but also in changing their body chemistry. This is done by our thoughts, reverberating around in our minds and affecting our bodies. We sort of know this intuitively, but we make the wrong decisions, or fail to use it. We expect to be healed from some miracle from the 'outside,' rather than from the 'inside.' "

Finally, I suggested she practice imaging the army of white blood cells, led by Jesus Christ, devouring the cancer cells, just as I did. "I know it will work for you," I wrote, "all you have to do is *believe*."

I received a very thoughtful letter from a woman I'll call Susan, from Valley Forge, Pennsylvania. How Susan wanted to believe that healing was possible! Her problem, though, was *how* to latch onto faith, or as she put it, ". . . how to gain that conviction of deliverance which starts or immediately accomplishes the healing. [This] is something I have not learned—although I think I have read virtually everything on the subject." She went on: ". . . I gather that you simply *determined* to believe. . . . It's as though you resolved to believe as [Milly Gordon and Lew Miller] did—and that you then were able to do it . . . your *determination* to believe (rather than a sudden unaccountable happening) enabled you to believe. This seems to me a new thought, and I find hope in it.

"I hope and pray that I can do it. Goodness knows, I've tried everything else, and I'm willing indeed to grasp even at straws."

Straws? In my reply I wrote in part:

"Our Lord in His mercy understands our struggle for faith. . . . As for the prayer of faith, it is a simple thing. It is talking to God as you would talk to your own earthly father, with implicit trust in His love for you and with unfaltering confidence in His personal concern for your welfare. It is knowing in your heart what you say with your lips.

"I found that my mind had to be first satisfied with the concept of the healing Christ *before* I could take that final step which led to my heart's acceptance of Him. The prayer resulting from the joining of my *mind's* belief and my *heart's* faith was the means by which His power was set free in my life.

"I would say that this explains, to the best of my ability, the *how* of faith.

"Susan, I sincerely trust that you find your faith. Remember, every thought is a prayer. And may Jesus Christ come into your life as He did into mine. 'Ye shall . . . find me, when ye shall search for me with all your heart' (Jeremiah 29:13)."

Not all my correspondence is so uplifting. One woman wrote from a southern state that her father had a malignancy that had resulted in the removal of a section of his intestines. The disease had then attacked other organs. "Medically speaking his chances of survival are just about nil," she wrote.

"After showing [your] article to my father, he read it, but . . . has some reservations, based on the medical validity of the account of your cancer cure. Dad has considerable medical experience, having worked in hospital-type laboratories. . . .

"Admittedly, he takes the rationalist approach to religion, which he has been studying as long as I have known him. As I see it, the only hope Dad has is a belief in a loving God who is still in the healing business today, as your testimony assures us.

"Is there some way that we could substantiate that you actually had cancer and that it is now gone? Any help you can provide will be appreciated."

Here are excerpts from my reply:

"I really do not know how to answer your letter. What you are saying is, 'Harry DeCamp never had cancer, because cancer *must* kill.' You are also telling me your father has no faith in God. He believes 'Cancer-power' is stronger than 'God-power.' I must advise you that if this is the way your father believes, so it will be. There is really nothing I can do for him.

"In defense of 'God-power,' however, let me say that I had every test known to the medical profession. I was cut open *twice* from my breastbone to my pelvic bone by two specialists, including one from Sloan-Kettering in New York. Both doctors stated that the cancer had spread so extensively throughout the body tissue that surgery was impossible. They advised my family and myself that there was no hope whatsoever.

"Perhaps that is not proof enough for your father, but it sure was proof enough for me! I'm overjoyed that God healed my cancer. All X rays, scans, and blood tests show no signs of cancer, either in the blood, the bone or in the body tissue. The mass which was behind my bladder has gone. . . .

"If your father would open his heart to God, he just might find Him there, ready to help. I will pray for your father, and ask that the Holy Spirit will come into him as He came into me during my trials. . . .

"May God bless you both. . . ."

Tough talk? Sure. But I believe that confrontation, in love, is sometimes necessary to shake people out of their unbelief.

I sometimes find, particularly with phone calls, that even after they have read my story and know my views, people don't really want to talk about healing at all. Strange. They want to talk instead about the kind of cancer they have, what treatments they are taking and how much they are suffering. They seem so wrapped up in self-analysis and self-pity that they actually enjoy it.

I tell them that I am sorry but I am not interested in talking about the details of their cancer. I say, "I want to talk to you about your healing, not your cancer. You've been so brainwashed by the media into believing that because you have cancer you will die, that you *are* going to die."

They react to this with shock. (I can't blame them!) "That's a fine way to speak!" they'll say, or words to that effect.

"I'm sorry," I reply, "but *you* called me. You *say* you want me to tell you how I beat cancer, but you're not really listening. All you want to do is talk about your symptoms. I think you're going about this in the wrong way."

Happily, there are those who are willing to step out in faith. At least six people who have written to me have since written again, or called, to say that they have put faith and imaging into practice and have been healed. Two of them had cancer.

One of the two is a woman, whom I'll call Maggie, from Virginia. Maggie still calls Bess and me from time to time. When we began corresponding she had been in bed for two years in great agony, slowly wasting away from cancer of the spine. She confessed that the thing she missed the most was not being able to wear high heels.

After she put her faith to work, Maggie began to get better. Eventually she got out of bed and began to do her housework. Then she got dressed and went to church to thank God for her healing. *She was wearing her high heels.*

I need to hear some happy endings. The responsibility I have is great. Does that sound self-important? I hope not; I don't mean it to be. You might ask how it is that a layman such as I has the effrontery, the nerve, to talk and write to people not only about cancer but about spiritual matters. After all, I am a simple man with only a high school education; I've never been near a medical school, and all I know of theology is what I read in the Bible.

It is not my work to speak as a medical or spiritual authority, for I am, quite clearly, neither. I try to be careful about that. The only reason I can do what I am doing *at all* is that I know *beyond a doubt* that God healed me, and I sincerely believe that He wants me to be a messenger to spread the news that through Him even cancer patients can have life, not death.

Frankly I don't think that faith or healing has anything to do with whether a man is ordained or not. I could have studied all about theology and religious doctrine, and have a string of degrees as long as your arm, but none of this could have given me that *feeling* I experienced when God touched me with His healing power. That was an unearned, unmerited gift.

Theologians help us by explaining or constructing doctrines that state intellectually the why and how of God and His power. But explanations and doctrine have nothing to do with the actual *experience* of that power. That can come to anyone: a shepherd, a fisherman, or even a businessman from West Long Branch.

Christ said, "Truly, truly, I say to you, he who believes in me will also do the works that I do; and greater works than these will he do, because I go to the Father" (John 14:12 RSV). I believe Our Lord was talking not only to those with Him in the upper room, but to anyone who has the faith to believe. He was talking to *you*; He was talking to *me*. That is why I can talk to cancer patients and even engage learned ministers in discussion about healing through faith.

Yet I feel it is no contradiction to say that the whole business makes me feel almost *inferior.* The responsibility is almost frightening. I feel I can't handle such a big job; I'm not able to. The only way I can do it at all is to simply go ahead and get on with it—trusting God in me to make it all work out right. And so far it *is* working.

If I seem to have been overly hard on doctors and hospitals in this book, let me say again that I believe God gave us doctors and medicine, and we are to use them. They are gifts from a good and loving Father. But consider this: doctors (and hospitals) only create a climate in which we can be healed. No doctor has ever "healed" a simple finger cut. He only cleans it, puts medication on it, or stitches it. It is God alone, through the miraculous mechanism of cell renewal, who does the healing.

Centuries ago, before the rise of modern science, I understand that faith healing was commonplace. With the advent of science, prayer and faith as a means of healing fell into disuse. Science provided man with a "quick fix" for all the ills that flesh is heir to. So today, people have come to depend more on science than on God. In fact, in this "post-Christian" era, for most people God has just faded out of the picture. This is very sad.

Today, however, we are seeing a renewal of the practice of healing through faith in the churches—including the Roman Catholic Church and the Protestant denominations. God's healing power has always been available, but until recently the churches have been slow to pick up on it.

What can I say to you who may have been given the death sentence of cancer? What can I say to comfort you, to *convince* you that there *is* hope?

Consider my case: When I was given the same death sentence back in 1976, I didn't have someone telling me there was hope. For me, there was no way out, none whatsoever. You, at least, have this book in your hand, offering you hope, *if you can believe.*

For many months, I opened every door in a futile, desperate search for healing. It was always the next doctor, the next procedure, the next treatment, that was going to save me. But every door led to a hallway that was a deadend. The one door that I didn't open was the door to belief. When I lay dying—almost at the last minute—I was given the key to that door, when I read those two stories in *Guideposts.* Hopefully you won't have to wait that long. You can start believing today, *now.*

For most of us, I think, the root of the problem is that we *say* we believe. *But we really don't believe.* I may be misunderstood for suggesting this, but I sincerely think that in approaching the subject of nonmedical healing, we must let our intellects go by the board, because they are blocking true belief.

There is a great mystery, a paradox here. After all, God gave us minds with which to think; He has put within us the capacity and curiosity to learn. Both Judaism and Christianity at their best have fostered learning and the getting of wisdom.

Be that as it may, I think our intellect is the greatest stumbling block to healing through faith. We feel we must explain and justify *everything* intellectually. This is the heritage of scientific materialism. In our pride—our *arrogance*—we think that our finite minds must understand the processes by which everything works; and if we cannot understand a thing then we will not accept it.

If you are suffering from cancer or any other serious illness, and the doctors have given up on you, you have actually reached the end of the line, as far as physical science, knowledge, and intellectualizing go. The doctors have done all this already for you; they have come to the end of their resources. They are, after all, only men. So intellectualizing about a cure has failed.

I believe that you must now forget all that (since it hasn't worked anyway) and revert back to the kind of belief you had when you were a child, which has nothing to do with intellectualism.

Remember the way you once believed in Santa Claus? *That* is the way you must believe in God now, if you are going to be healed.

You doubt me? OK! Don't take my word for it. Listen instead to the words of Jesus Himself: "Truly, I say to you, unless you turn and become like children, you will never enter the kingdom of heaven" (Matthew 18:3 RSV).

Please, think about the implications of that verse. Jesus is not suggesting that we put the good brains God gave us on hold, so to speak. But He *is* asking us to adopt an attitude of total trust in God—just as a little child does with Santa Claus or Daddy.

My friends, there is magic in believing. And God *will* listen to you, when you stop trying to force His hand, when you stop trying to look at your illness "intelligently." You must let God take over. The way you do that is to mentally step back and just say, "Thank You, God, for healing me." And you *know* it's done; you *believe* it's done.

I think what I am trying to say can be summed up in the words of Jesus, words which I've quoted before in this book. My friend, if you can't believe anything *I* have told you, please believe Jesus Christ, the Author of all truth: *"Therefore I tell you, whatever you ask in prayer, believe that you receive it, and you will"* (Mark 11:24 RSV).

9

What to Do if You—or Someone You Love—Has Cancer

"I waited patiently for the Lord, and he inclined unto me, and heard my cry. He brought me up also out of an horrible pit, out of the miry clay, and set my feet upon a rock, and established my goings. And he hath put a new song in my mouth, even praise unto our God. . . ."

Psalms 40:1–3

I have discovered that there's a reason for God holding me to my promise to shout His praises from the housetops. People have needed to hear that there is hope, just as I so desperately needed help, sitting there through endless days, staring at the TV, slowly dying of cancer. Now hardly a day goes by but that someone with a "hopeless" condition—it may be cancer or it may be something else—calls or writes to me, asking my help. In this book I have tried to explain how God healed me and what I say to such people. It may be helpful now for me to summarize what I tell these people so that others who pick up this book may also be helped. This is my prayer.

If you or a loved one is facing cancer or any life-threatening disease or dilemma, I counsel you to seek *the way out.* Help will come. Healing can come, but you must seek it.

"How?"—you ask.

I would answer that with one word above all else. *Believe!* Reading how God healed Lew Miller and Milly Gordon helped me begin to believe that He could heal me. Because God healed me I know that He can heal you or the one you love. But you must believe it to be healed.

However, since you may not be able to believe just yet, and because there are other things you can do—and one thing you should not do!—I will suggest some steps for you and your loved ones to take. Then I will discuss each one briefly.

1. **Face the problem honestly.**
2. **Do not give way to fear and panic.**
3. **Believe God's power is the strongest force in the universe.**
4. **Surrender yourself to God's holy will.**
5. **Affirm your healing.**
6. **Continue medical treatment.**
7. **Thank God for your healing.**
8. **Tell others.**

1. Face the problem honestly.

The first step toward healing is to face your cancer honestly. We humans are masters at rationalization and denial, particularly when it comes to admitting to facts that are unpleasant. Healing does not come from a blind, rigid denial of the facts. On the contrary, the only way to deal with an enemy like cancer is to see it for what it is. It will actually help you to tell yourself, "I have cancer."

If cancer has struck one you love, you can help that person perhaps more at this point than any other by simply talking about the cancer (and using the *word*) in a natural way. Of course, you will not be casual or flippant, but you will want to avoid the other extreme. Don't be *grimly* honest. Just accept it as the physician's diagnosis, unless peculiar circumstances should lead you to seek another professional opinion. Your acceptance of the harsh reality will greatly help your friend to face it honestly also.

2. Do not give way to fear and panic.

To say to himself *I have cancer* may frighten the patient. At first he will probably tremble and cry when he tells those nearest and dearest to him. He may become angry. That is all right. He is realizing the severity of the problem.

But there is one thing the patient will *not* want to do. *Don't be afraid.* I am told that there are at least 365 *fear nots* in the Bible. One for every day of the year! When I first learned that I had cancer, I was very afraid. And I didn't know about all those *fear nots.* Most people are afraid when they are told the bad news. And fear can lead to panic, which is loss of control.

If you have cancer, realize that to a large degree what frightens you is the very word itself. We have been brainwashed into believing that *cancer* and *death* are synonymous. For years, people automatically concluded that if they had cancer they would die. Thankfully, with advances in medicine, this is beginning to change.

Kal Eisenbud, whom I have mentioned in this book, gave Bess and me the best advice when he told us not to be afraid to say the word cancer. "Bring it out of the closet and talk about it," Kal advised. Bess and I did this and I think that is why cancer did not gain such a dreaded grip on me. I know that I am giving you truthful counsel when I tell you not to be afraid, for some of the most frequent words on Jesus' lips were "FEAR NOT."

3. Believe God's power is the strongest force in the universe.

God's power is stronger than Cancer power. Having accepted this, it seems logical to me that if anyone wants to be healed of something as serious as cancer he must put himself in God's care. God is the King of all creation. He created our bodies and He alone can heal them.

There is a strange idea that is still very much with us that says that since sickness is a result of the fallen creation, we must suffer it patiently. It is part of the price we pay as children of Adam and Eve. I think this notion is contrary to the spirit of the New Testament. If you read the Gospels, you will find that Jesus gladly healed every single person who came to Him. He never told anyone that they were to accept their illness. And He treated blindness, paralysis, leprosy—even death—all alike, as if they were enemies to be vanquished. And He is the Healer today, too. Believe that God in Christ is all powerful. And believe that God in Christ loves you and does not want you sick.

I have quoted one verse several times in this book. It was like a life preserver to me, and it can be to you, if you will learn it and think upon it and claim it as a promise from God for you. Memorize this verse:

> Therefore I tell you, whatever you ask in prayer,
> believe that you receive it, and you will.
>
> Mark 11:24 RSV

In addition to this, turn back to page 141 of this book and read again what I have said about simple faith. Belief is the key!

4. Surrender yourself to God's holy will.

This may be the most difficult "medicine" for the patient to take. I am not saying to lie down and give up. That is not what I am saying at all.

The cancer victim may feel right now that God is his enemy, but on the contrary He is the greatest Friend. It will do no good to resist Him or to fight against Him. He only wants what is best for us, so why should we not surrender to His plan?

Think of what a mother does. She loves her child and wants to protect him from all suffering. But she knows that one day this child needs to be independent of her, able to stand on his own two feet. Taking her child to nursery school and leaving him there is one step in that direction and although the child may cry and feel abandoned, she does take him and leave him—though he is never far from her loving thoughts—so that he may grow. She allows the temporary hurt so that she may accomplish a higher purpose.

I believe that it is the same with God. He may allow us to suffer for a while, but we must believe that because He loves us, our suffering will somehow work for our ultimate good. In my case, before my cancer I was a self-satisfied irreligious man. It took cancer to bring me to God. I can say to you, therefore, place yourself in the perfect will of God, without reservation, and believe Him even for the grace to do that. He will supply the grace without fail.

5. Affirm your healing.

Your next step is to affirm your healing. This is your right and privilege. Using all of the resources at your command—the Bible, prayer, talking with Christian friends, "imaging"—*affirm your healing.*

Begin to image or visualize your healing in your mind. Remember, imaging is a form of prayer. Use whatever images are best for you. (One little boy who had cancer drew pictures of himself shooting his cancer, which resembled a large, very ugly potato, with a squirt gun. The boy got better.)

I found the device of a little TV screen in my head most effective. If you think this would work for you too, on the screen "see" the white cells, marching like an army through your body, devouring the cancer cells. It is not important what the cells actually look like. Imagine them any way you please. The Pac-man is a handy new model. Picture little Pac-men gobbling up the cancer cells.

I imaged the white cells massing at my shoulders. Then, with a tiny Jesus Christ leading the charge, they would sweep down into my stomach, then battle their way into my liver, my heart, my lungs, and especially, my bladder. Thousands upon thousands of those brave little white cells would move in, devouring those ugly, evil cancer cells. Then the victorious "white army," led by the Savior would move down into my legs, feet, and toes. Reversing themselves, they would sweep up again through my body, mopping up stray cancer cells as they went until at last the battle was won and Jesus Christ stood victorious.

It is very important to replay the scene over and over and over. Repetition will impress the images into your subconscious mind and make those images a part of you. This will take time, but keep at it. I suggest you set aside definite blocks of time—at morning, midday and evening, and before going to sleep—for imaging your healing. But you need not limit yourself to these times. You may find the images flashing on your mental TV screen at odd moments during the day. If they do, let it roll.

6. Continue medical treatment.

I would caution anyone who is seeking healing *not* to stop medical treatment. When God healed me, I felt it in the depth of my being. Since I knew I was healed, I did not want to take chemotherapy, but I took it anyway—simply to please Bess and my doctor.

God has given us doctors and medicine to help us. They are good gifts and we are to use them. Not to use them, I believe, is to tempt God.

You may remember in the Bible how Satan tempted Christ to throw Himself down from the pinnacle of the temple. Satan even quoted Scripture to our Lord: " 'He will give his angels charge of you . . . On their hands they will bear you up, lest you strike your foot against a stone' " (Matthew 4:6 RSV).

Christ, of course, knew that God *could* send an angel to bear Him up, but He replied: "Again it is written, 'You shall not tempt the Lord your God.' " By the same token, when we are gravely ill I think it is tempting God to refuse medical treatment. *I feel that doctors provide the treatments and God supplies the healing.*

The particular way God healed Harry DeCamp may not be the way He will heal you. It would be wrong for anyone to slavishly imitate what I did. My advice is to utilize every means known to science, along with generous doses of faith and prayer, to bring about healing!

7. Thank God for your healing.

It is a sign of faith and trust in God to thank Him for your healing *before it occurs.* This is not presumption; it is faith. Remember the words of Scripture: "Faith is the substance of things hoped for, the evidence of things not seen" (Hebrews 11:1).

Faith is believing when you haven't yet seen the results. It is not blind belief, though. It is trusting that God loves you and wants you to be whole and well, as He created you to be. When you thank God for your healing while you are still sick, you are saying in essence, "God, I believe I will be well again in Your time, however long that takes. To show you I believe that, I am thanking You in advance."

Thanking God for your healing also affirms the fact of the healing for you, impresses it on your mind and subconscious, eventually making it a reality. *Thanking God in advance for your healing is a way of thinking and acting as if your healing is already a fact.* In my case, I prayed constantly for weeks, thanking God for my healing every day, though I was still sick. Finally, one day, when I was in the act of thanking God for the healing *that had not yet occurred,* I suddenly felt the actual healing take place in my body.

8. Tell others.

When you are healed, no one will have to tell you to talk about it. You will . . . and you should! Give God the credit.

But do not be surprised if your doctor, or even your family, does not immediately believe you. Ninety-nine and nine-tenths percent of all doctors do not appear to go along with any type of faith healing. That is their privilege. You will know, though, that God healed you because you have experienced it in the depth of your being, as I have. You will need no one to tell you that you are healed or who was responsible for it.

Recognize the fact that others—including your doctor, your family, and your friends—have not felt God touch *them* with His healing power. *They* have not had the experience. *You* have. So, you cannot expect them to believe you at first. Later, when you are getting stronger, gaining weight, getting out of bed, they may believe you. Then again, they may put it down to "remission."

Let them think what they please. Simply continue to tell them that you are healed and that God is the One who healed you. Don't ever apologize for giving God the credit. Remember the words of Jesus: "For whoever is ashamed of me . . . of him will the Son of Man be ashamed when he comes in his glory and the glory of the Father and of the holy angels" (Luke 9:26).

In conclusion, I must say a word about those who are not healed. Earlier, I used the analogy of gold—if everyone had it, it would have no value. If everyone were healed, then healings would no longer be miraculous.

The Bible says, ". . . it is appointed unto men once to die . . ." (Hebrews 9:27). All of us have to die, sooner or later. God has given doctors the knowledge to increase our life expectancy, and this is wonderful. Yet, we must all die, whether we live to be fifty or a hundred. Our faith in God will make the transition much easier.

We place such importance on this present life—a life that

lasts but seventy or eighty years for most of us. Christianity teaches us, however, that this mortal life is just a prelude to eternal life in heaven with God.

If we really believe this, as we say we do, we won't think it such an utter, crushing tragedy when we must die at fifty-five or sixty-five—or even at five. Remember the words of Paul: "What no eye has seen, nor ear heard, nor the heart of man conceived, . . . God has prepared for those who love him" (1 Corinthians 2:9 RSV).

Given the fact of death, the inevitable, inescapable fact that we must one day die, God has placed within all of us a healthy desire to stay alive as long as possible. As children of our loving Heavenly Father it is our right to ask for life and health when we are sick. I asked for it, and God heard me and gave me back my life when I was at death's very door. And if He did that for me, an ordinary Joe, He will do it for you, too. All you have to do is *believe.*